PENGUIN CLASSICS

STRINDBERG: THREE PLAYS

August Strindberg, born in Stockholm in 1849, was the author of more than fifty plays, as well as novels, short stories, poems and an autobiography. Few of his earlier plays are remembered, but from the 1880s his writing took on the intensity which characterizes such plays as *The Father* and *Miss Julie*. He went on to write historical dramas based on Swedish history and a series of plays dealing with similar themes to those of his middle period, including *Easter* and *The Dance of Death*. He died in 1912.

Peter Watts also translated *Ghosts and Other Plays* by Henrik Ibsen for the Penguin Classics. While working at the BBC as a drama producer, he produced most of his translations of Ibsen and Strindberg on the Third Programme. He died in 1972.

90000975 WJB

THREE PLAYS

August Strindberg

★

THE FATHER
MISS JULIA
EASTER

Translated by
PETER WATTS

PENGUIN BOOKS

PENGUIN BOOKS

Published by the Penguin Group
27 Wrights Lane, London W8 5TZ, England
Viking Penguin Inc., 40 West 23rd Street, New York, New York 10010, USA
Penguin Books Australia Ltd, Ringwood, Victoria, Australia
Penguin Books Canada Ltd, 2801 John Street, Markham, Ontario, Canada L3R 1B4
Penguin Books (NZ) Ltd, 182–190 Wairau Road, Auckland 10, New Zealand

Penguin Books Ltd, Registered Offices: Harmondsworth, Middlesex, England

This translation first published 1958
17 19 20 18

All applications for licences to perform plays in this volume should
be made to A. P. Watts & Son, 26/28 Bedford Row,
London WC1R 4HL

Made and printed in Great Britain by
Hazell Watson & Viney Limited
Member of BPCC Limited
Aylesbury, Bucks, England
Set in Monotype Perpetua

CONTENTS

INTRODUCTION

ALTHOUGH August Strindberg, in his sixty-three years from 1849 to 1912, produced a vast volume of work – ranging from short stories, poems, and autobiographical novels, to Utopian essays and treatises on chemistry and semantics – it is on his plays that nearly all his fame rests. These fall into well-defined categories, corresponding roughly with the different periods of his life: (1) Early Work; (2) Children's Plays – to which he was inclined to return in his few happier moments; (3) Realistic Plays – a revolt against the stuffy theatrical conventions of his day, and largely occasioned by his turbulent relations with his first wife; (4) the Historical Cycle, written at various times throughout his life, usually after a period of particular turmoil, when he may have found it a relief to escape into the past; (5) the Mystical Plays, which came late in his life when he began to find comfort in religion; and finally (6) what he called his 'Chamber Plays', written for the intimate Strindberg Theatre in Stockholm.

Of the three plays in this book, two – *The Father* and *Miss Julia* – belong to his Realistic period; while *Easter*, written twelve years later, is the most naturalistic of the Mystical Plays.

Since, even more than most authors, Strindberg wrote his personal experiences and mental processes into all his work – often in contexts where they seem barely relevant – a short outline of his life might help readers to understand and appreciate even such comparatively simple plays as these.

He was born, prematurely and unwanted, in Stockholm in 1849, four months after his father, a shipping agent of good family, had married his mother, a servant girl who had already borne him three children. At the time of his birth his father had just gone bankrupt, and for much of his childhood August Strindberg suffered from poverty and hunger; and as his mother had twelve children in all, the house must have been unbearably overcrowded. Strindberg adored his mother, but though she was proud of his quick and vital intelligence, he could never become her favourite however much he struggled to win her love. Much of his fantastic energy was squandered on trying to impress her; one of his brothers drew well, so August set himself to draw better; another, Axel, played the piano, and since August could never bring himself to submit to the discipline or drudgery of practising enough to play well, he made himself something of an authority on musical theory and technique. He would concentrate on a subject till he had mastered it (or could convince himself that he had) and then lose all interest in it. He was also a strong swimmer, a passable rider, and a good shot.

When he was thirteen his mother died, and within the year his father married again – their young housekeeper. Much of Strindberg's writing shows the scars of the humiliations that this woman devised for him, and though he unconsciously built his wrongs up into something monstrous – as throughout his life he was apt to do with any rebuff or rejection – there is no doubt that she gave him cause enough. By this time he was in a continual state of revolt against the established order wherever he encountered it – a state of mind that did not make either his schooldays or his time at Uppsala University either happy or easy. Added to this, in his struggle with poverty he had to take on all kinds of jobs, from teaching to journalism and acting. His career as an actor was short and inglorious. Dissatisfied with the walk-on parts that he was given, he demanded a leading role, but when eventually he badgered the management into giving him one, he failed so ignominiously that he tried to kill himself. His next part was that of prompter. But at any rate he had gained first-hand theatrical experience that was invaluable when he came to write his plays.

He was twenty when he wrote his first play – a comedy called *The Birthday Gift*, which he wrote in four days. His friends, when he read it to them, hailed him as a genius, and that night he thanked God on his knees. The Director of the theatre, in rejecting it, admitted that it had merit, and Strindberg, fired by this encouragement, settled down to write a play on ancient Greece (which was also rejected) and a Passion Play – which he burned in its early stages. He next tried a verse play on the Danish sculptor Thorwaldsen, which was produced by the Royal Theatre in 1870. On the first night he was horrified, and ran sobbing from the theatre to deaden his humiliation in drink. While waiting for production, he had written a prose drama, *The Free Thinker*, which was his first work to be published; the critics' strictures on it only spurred him to embark on a grander work on the same theme, with a Viking setting – the first of his historical plays. *The Outlaw* was staged without much success, and Strindberg was now penniless again. One day there came a summons to the Royal Palace; King Karl XV had seen *The Outlaw* and liked it enough to promise Strindberg a quarterly stipend from the

Privy Purse till he had finished his studies at the university. Unfortunately for his high hopes, after two payments the royal bounty inexplicably ceased. Strindberg – apart from his usual reaction that enemies were plotting behind his back – was almost relieved. He now felt free and, leaving the university, he returned to Stockholm full of wonderful hopes and plans.

With his fierce energy he was ready to turn his hand to almost anything; painting, journalism, medicine. He now became an *habitué* of the Red Room, the meeting-place in a Stockholm restaurant of advanced artists and writers. Their life was consciously Bohemian, and Strindberg followed the pattern with drink and women. Throughout his life he was tormented with guilt about sex, but in spite of savage fits of remorse, he was always at the mercy of his desires. Perhaps that was why, whatever mistresses and casual affairs he might have, he tended to fall in *love* with apparently unattainable innocent child-like girls. Always at the back of his mind was the Madonna-like figure into which he had idealized the dead mother who had never given him the love that he longed for.

In the summer of 1872 the paper for which he was then working closed down, and Strindberg, feeling free again, retired to the seaside at Kymmendö to write a historical drama, *Master Olaf*, on the hero of the Swedish Reformation. Here he was happy, and his stepmother and two of his sisters came to stay with him. But the play was rejected, and Strindberg became both physically and mentally ill.

He recovered to find himself wretchedly poor again, and he lived by journalism and tutoring. He even took a post in the Royal Library, where he volunteered to catalogue the Chinese Manuscripts – learning enough Chinese for the purpose in a year to be accepted as an authority on that complicated language.

When he was twenty-six he met Siri von Essen, the wife of a Guards officer, Baron Wrangel. She was his ideal, fair-haired and blue-eyed, with the face of a child, although she was already a mother. When Strindberg saw her with her daughter in her arms he was captivated as never before – though in fact Siri's maternal instincts were not as strong as he liked to believe. He became a frequent visitor at their house – which, strangely enough, was one where he had spent much of his childhood – and the three became firm friends. Perhaps the Baron always knew of Strindberg's love for his wife (which Strindberg convinced himself was purely spiritual); perhaps he did not mind, for he was openly unfaithful to her. Strindberg was horrified at the idea of this innocent creature submitting to the Baron's embraces, and at last, after another attempt at suicide (by pneumonia, this time!) he confessed his love. After a show of surprise on her part, they became lovers. The Baron seemed content with the situation until the scandal threatened his family name; then he divorced Siri on the technical grounds of desertion, the ostensible reason being that she wanted to go on the stage, which was impossible for the wife of a Guards officer. Soon she made quite a success, and was earning more than Strindberg, whose energies had been devoted to rewriting *Master Olaf* in verse, only to have it rejected yet again. He grew bitter, and reproached himself endlessly that their love was physical rather than spiritual. After an unsatisfactory year of the free love that Strindberg believed in so rebelliously, Siri found herself pregnant. He was overjoyed, and insisted on marriage both for the child's sake and to wipe out the squalor and shame of the illicit union to which his principles had condemned him. They were married at the end of 1877 and a period of great happiness began for both of them, in spite of the premature birth and death of the child. Strindberg published a successful book of short stories of university life, *Town and Gown*; but though *Master Olaf* found a publisher shortly afterwards, the critics ignored it. Now that he was happy and living in comfort he was able to write more freely, and the following year his autobiographical novel, *The Red Room*, a savage attack on the state of Swedish society, appeared and ran into two editions at once. Strindberg was at last an accepted author. In the next two years Siri bore him two daughters to whom he was devoted. All his debts were paid and, what was more, the original version of *Master Olaf*, after nine years, was successfully produced. He was so happy that he set all his other work aside to write, in a fortnight, a delightful fairy play, *Lucky Peter's Travels*, which was accepted for production at once. Next he wrote a play for Siri's return to the stage. This play, *The Wife of Herr Bengt*, was Strindberg's personal answer to Ibsen's *A Doll's House* – which he hated – in which love finally triumphed over all marital disagreements. There was also a good deal of wishful thinking in it, for, much as he loved marriage and parenthood, Siri's extravagance, her slovenliness in the home, and the charm which in public she turned on so indiscriminately, had all by now come to infuriate him.

For the next four years Strindberg deserted the theatre, and wrote at bitter length of Sweden's past and present, and what he felt should be her future. However, the work that caused most stir was a two-volume collection of short stories called *Married*, exploring the difficulties and frustrations of wedded life; these – although he assured Siri that the couples he caricatured were entirely imaginary – were largely autobiographical. However, although we are accustomed to think of all Strindberg's relations with women as transitory and unhappy, his marriage to Siri was to last for nearly fourteen years; and, stormy though parts of it were, it is interesting and surprising to learn that, on one anniversary at about this time, Siri was able to raise her glass to him and thank him for seven happy years of married life.

In 1883 that marriage passed through one of its more difficult passages. Strindberg was jealous of Siri's very moderate success as an actress, of anyone of whom she seemed fond – even her little dog – and particularly of a woman friend whom, on the plea of economy, she had invited to share their home. So upset did he become that his doctor prescribed travel if he was to avert a nervous breakdown. Taking the children and the loathed little dog, they went first to Paris, and then through Italy to Switzerland, where their third child, Hans, was born.

Then came the news that the publication of the first volume of *Married* in Sweden had brought a charge of blasphemy, and at last Strindberg decided to go back to Stockholm, rather than let his publisher face the charge alone. He spent much of the journey in tears, expecting at least the two years imprisonment the Swedish law demanded. To his amazement, his train was met at Stockholm by a crowd of young writers and artists who hailed him as their leader. His hotel room was filled with flowers, and a gala performance of *Lucky Peter* was given in his honour; and when at last the charge against him failed, a medal was struck to celebrate his triumph. However, mistrusting the fickle loyalty of the crowd, he hurried back to Siri in Switzerland. He was convinced that the Feminists had been behind his trial, and for years afterwards he would blame their plots for every misfortune that overtook him.

Poverty once again made life difficult for the family, and the arrival of a Danish girl, Marie David, short-haired and emancipated, brought a fresh strain to the marriage. From Siri's delight in her company, and the trouble she suddenly began to take with her appearance, Strindberg became convinced that the girls were lovers – indeed that, while he had been strictly faithful during their marriage, Siri had been having affairs with both men and women. He began to inquire into her past; he would make long unexplained journeys to find evidence of her guilt, then would come back and fall at her feet and beg forgiveness. The stresses of this period drove him to write a series of autobiographical novels, ranging from his childhood (*The Son of a Maidservant*) to his maturity (*The Writer*). These books, though not always strictly accurate, or even consistent, give a unique and terrifying account of the development of a genius. He gradually found, though, that it was in dramatic form that he could best draw character, and he set out to write two naturalistic plays about marriage. The first, *The Marauders*, which he later ironically renamed *Comrades*, told of the ruthless battle for supremacy in the home between a couple who were both artists. This play – it is not a very good one – was rejected, and he flung his whole energy into a play on the themes that were surging in his mind – woman's ruthlessness in the struggle between man and wife, jealousy and paternity, and his nagging fear that his mind was going.

The Father was an immediate success, and on its first production in Copenhagen, Strindberg was hailed as a genius. But his marriage was now finally breaking up; he had already left Siri more than once, but had always returned, finding that he could not live without her. Now, at last, the torment of being with her had come to outweigh the pain of separation, and he tried, unsuccessfully, for a divorce. By this time he was working on the fifth volume of his autobiography, *A Fool's Defence*. This was a savage and unrestrained attack on Siri, accusing her of infidelity and perversion. He wrote it in French, 'to ensure that it should be widely read' (though later, when he grew ashamed of the book, he was to deny that he ever meant it to be published at all).

The following year he wrote *Miss Julia*, artistically the most successful of his experiments in naturalism. It was produced abroad and attacked by the critics, and it was twenty-five years before it was seen on the stage in his native land. Next followed a series of plays, of which *Creditors* is probably the best known; they are mostly in one act and none of any great value. They were written for the Théâtre Libre in Paris, and Siri, in spite of their domestic troubles, was to play the leading part.

In 1891 he and Siri were divorced at last. Though she was very drunk when she came before the tribunal, she was given custody of the three children – which was a bitter blow to Strindberg. After the divorce, Siri went to live in Finland with Marie David.

Strindberg now felt himself completely lost. He could not write, his children were gone, and his hopes of a Strindberg Theatre had failed.

He tried to paint again, but his pictures brought in only enough to pay for drink. He quarrelled with most of his friends – his ingrained persecution mania convincing him that they had turned against him – and his hair went grey. He decided that his real *métier* was science, and, rebelling against current scientific opinion, became fascinated with the idea that certain so-called elements – notably sulphur – were capable of further splitting. Only his lack of money for experiments, he was sure, hindered him from springing great discoveries on the world.

Eventually, the few friends left to him organized a public subscription – much to his fury – which paid for him to go to Berlin, where they nursed him back to something approaching mental and physical health.

In 1893 Strindberg astonished his Berlin circle by giving up his somewhat Bohemian life and marrying Frida Uhl, a young authoress of good Austrian family. They were married in Heligoland, under English law, and spent most of their honeymoon in England. London was sweltering under a heat-wave, and here Strindberg began to have the hallucinations that were to obsess him for the next few years; once, as he was crossing Waterloo Bridge, he suddenly felt that all the beggars in London were converging on him like giants. After two months he went back to Germany, leaving Frida behind, ostensibly to arrange for the English production of his plays. But the marriage was not a success; he had always wanted Siri to write rather than act, but now that he was married to a writer he found himself jealous and suspicious of her work. When, eventually, during a quarrel, Frida dared to question the worth of his writing, he had to leave her, and they lapsed into a long correspondence, full of illogical squabbling and inconsistent affection. By now Strindberg's mental state was beginning to alarm his friends. Eventually he went to stay with Frida's parents in Austria, but when there was a possibility of her joining him there, he fled to Berlin. Here, once again, they came together, but it was not a success; Strindberg was completely wrapped up in his chemical experiments and in other, most esoteric researches; he even convinced himself that he was able to leave his body. Frida was now pregnant, and she found both this mental atmosphere and the physical one (consisting largely of the fumes of sulphur) unbearable, and they quarrelled again. She went to stay with her grandparents at Dornach on the Danube, and wrote asking him to join her. Here they were reconciled yet again, perhaps under the influence of plenty of good food and no worries. The grandfather disapproved of Strindberg's researches, however, and they argued

interminably over the chemical theories in his treatise *Antibarbarus.*
Once again *A Fool's Defence* was to plague him with a threat of prosecu-
tion in Berlin. Strindberg, as a Swede, refused to appear, but the grandparents, furious at being involved in any way with the police, turned
him out of their house. However, they lent the impoverished couple
a cottage on the estate, where for two months they were happy again.
Then the child was born and there was a further wrangle about having
her baptized a Catholic. By the end of 1894 they had finally parted
and Strindberg was living alone in Paris with his experiments.

It had long been his ambition to have his plays performed in Paris
and now *The Father* was an enormous success (though all that Strindberg
made out of it was 300 francs!), and at one time there were six of his
plays running at once. The honour had come to him before it did to
Ibsen, of whom he was bitterly and contemptuously jealous. At any
other time he would have been overjoyed, but now all that he cared
about was proving that carbon could be isolated from pure sulphur.
Alone and in great poverty in his little room in the Quartier Latin, he
pursued his researches until his hands were burned and festering so that
his arms swelled till he could not even dress himself. His persecution
mania grew till he suspected even his best friends of conspiracy; he
feared poison in his food, and noxious gases that he felt his enemies were
pouring into his room. He was even convinced that the piano-playing
of a neighbour was a plot to interfere with the researches that obsessed
him. At last the Swedish Colony in Paris heard of his condition and
made a collection to pay his rent so that he could go to a hospital. When
he was discharged from hospital two months later, his findings were
published in *Le Temps*. Some scientists actually supported his theory
that sulphur was not a true element, but when he went further and
claimed to be able to transmute base minerals, particularly mercury,
into gold they rejected him. His other books during this period were
two botanical treatises, but their publication only brought him further
into debt. He was convinced that invisible powers (as well as the
Feminists) were at work to frustrate him; he even tried to use witch-
craft to bring Frida back to him. The climax came at two o'clock one
morning – the hour at which he felt that attacks on his life were always
made – when he was 'struck down by an electric current' that paralysed
him and held him to the ground. The next day he fled to Sweden, where
he submitted to treatment from a friend, Dr Eliasson, for insanity.

For a time his condition improved, but then he began to suspect the doctor of trying to steal his secret formula for gold-making. In September 1896 he broke off treatment and went to Frida's mother in Austria. She, a disciple of Swedenborg, did more than anyone else to cure him. Certainly she succeeded, as he said, in 'frightening him back to God'. In the end, however, they disagreed, and he returned to Sweden, to the little town of Lund, the scene of his short stories, *Legends* – and of his play *Easter* written years later. During his convalescence here he wrote the story of his madness in *Inferno* – a vivid and merciless self-portrait of a great intellect in the grip of insanity. As he grew better (though he was still subject to attacks from the 'electric girdle') he began to find Lund dull and provincial, and soon convinced himself that omens from the flight of birds were directing him to go back to Paris.

In Paris, however, he found it difficult to write, and for a time he planned to enter a monastery in Belgium, until he heard that the abbot had been deposed for immorality. After this, his urge to become a Catholic faded. But now, just when everyone had decided that he was finished as a writer, suddenly the gift returned to him, and words flooded from his pen; for the first time since the bitter, realistic plays of six years before, when the marriage with Siri von Essen was breaking up, he began to write for the theatre again, and *To Damascus* was the first of his mystical plays. This is a huge work in three parts, of which the first two were written in 1898, but the third not till six years later. It is the story of his spiritual development and his madness, told in symbolic terms. Much of this brilliant fantasy of self-revelation is hard to follow, especially without an intimate knowledge of Strindberg's own history. It is based largely on his marriage with Frida Uhl, but hints and incidents from his earlier life appear from time to time. Though many of these incidents are not fully digested into the structure of the play, and though a taint of unreality and even of madness are never far away, the play has a tremendous power through its sincerity, its deep feeling, and its wisdom.

His next play *Advent* was a mystical religious play on Swedenborgian lines, and it was followed by *There are Crimes and Crimes*, in which he worked out the idea that spiritual guilt, though not culpable according to human laws, must yet be punished by heaven. He finished it with the feeling that a great weight of guilt had been lifted from him.

On his fiftieth birthday the critics of all Europe, and not least his own country, paid tribute to him, and there was a gala performance of

Master Olaf in Stockholm. Now, inspired by Shakespeare's Histories, he decided to write a linked series of historical plays from his own country's story. Discarding the simplicity of his middle period, he poured out a cycle of crowded, colourful, jostling dramas. First the *Saga of the Volsungs* from the fourteenth century, then the story of the Vasa Dynasty that had started with *Master Olaf; Gustavus Vasa, Erik XIV*, and *Gustavus Adolphus*. He was happy writing them, spending the summer on Kymmendö, with his friends to stay with him, as well as his nephews and nieces and even his daughter Greta; and this happiness continually shows itself in the plays at this time. He cared little for historical accuracy and there was a streak of mysticism through them all, but if the influence of Shakespeare is a little too obvious, and if they demand too great a knowledge of Swedish history for foreigners to appreciate them fully, they still remain a magnificent achievement of historical drama that no modern writer has surpassed.

In 1900 he saw the Norwegian actress Harriet Bosse playing Puck and cast her at once for the difficult part of The Lady in the first two plays of *To Damascus*. (Part III was not yet projected and was not written till four years later.) She was young and petite, with the innocence that always attracted him; and though she was not really well cast in the part, she made quite a success. Immediately he began to write a part that would suit her better – that of Eleanora in *Easter*. This, his most tender play, is a return to his realistic method, but with mysticism shining through. It is a play of expiation and forgiveness, and it looked as if Strindberg himself might be moving from gloom into the sunlight. However, his black mood fell on him again, and his next play was the terrible *Dance of Death*. Harriet Bosse, to whom he sent the manuscript, was horrified at the contrast. But he was already at work on a folk-tale *The Bridal Crown*, full of trolls and sprites, and he turned straight from this to *Swanwhite*, another fairy romance in which love finally triumphs over all obstacles. For Strindberg had fallen in love with Harriet Bosse. But though she was flattered at having captivated Sweden's leading literary figure, and pleased that he should write such parts for her, it was a long time before she could bring herself to accept his offer of marriage. At last, however, she persuaded herself that her love could reconcile Strindberg with the world, and she accepted him. After a delay while his marriage to Frida Uhl was formally dissolved, they were finally married in the Spring of 1901.

Though he was working hard on two more Histories – *Engelbrech*

and *Charles XII* — once again Strindberg could not reconcile his high
ideals about love with the tiresome trivialities of living. Both Harriet
and he felt themselves trapped, and out of his unhappiness Strindberg
wrote *A Dream Play*, in which Indra's daughter comes down to earth to
look into men's complaints. She finds that, though there may be happiness on the surface, there is always misery and suffering at the heart of
things. Strindberg was convinced that *A Dream Play* was his best work,
and indeed, though it is extremely difficult both for any theatre to stage
and for an audience to follow, it has a strangely compelling quality.
Here, even more than in *To Damascus*, the characters represent various
facets of Strindberg's own self, and they merge and separate be-
wilderingly.

Next he returned to his historical cycle, with *Queen Christina* and
Gustavus III. Harriet gave birth to a daughter, and soon made the baby's
health an excuse to go with it to the country. Strindberg was alone
again. He wrote the third part of *To Damascus*, but after an unsatisfactory
play on Luther, *The Nightingale of Wittenborg*, he deserted the theatre
once again for his autobiographical books. For the third time he found
that though he couldn't live with the woman he loved, he couldn't live
without her, and he kept up a pathetic correspondence with Harriet,
and often visited her and their daughter. His bitter solitude is reflected
in his books at the time, and particularly in the savage *Black Banners*, a
virulent attack on the literary world of his day, and particularly on his
agent and former friend Geijerstam, who for many years had given
Strindberg good cause to be grateful. The book attacked Geijerstam's
honesty and business integrity, and even accused him of helping to
break up the marriage with Harriet Bosse; it was so violent that the unfortunate man hardly dared to show his face in Stockholm, and died
soon afterwards. Even Strindberg's high esteem as a writer could not
excuse this book, and he found himself attacked once again on all sides.

More and more he withdrew himself from society, living in great
discomfort, looked after by a succession of unsatisfactory housekeepers,
and losing himself in his writing; and by 1906 he was seeing practically
no one but Anne-Marie, his little daughter. He found refuge once
again in Swedenborg, and worked on a huge three-volume treatise on
his philosophy. But though he was sincerely sorry about *Black Banners*,
he could not forgive the critics who had attacked him. He saw himself
as suffering on behalf of the community, and the following year his book,
The Scapegoat, showed him as a patient saint redeeming the world by

taking its sins on himself. In his solitary existence he believed that he was in telepathic communication with his friends and neighbours, suffering with their illnesses and operations, and even going through the pains of childbirth with a woman in a nearby house.

Only the foundation of a Strindberg Theatre brought him from his retirement. His plays, successful in many European capitals, but rejected by Swedish theatres, were at last presented in Stockholm. Even *A Dream Play* was put on, with Harriet as Indra's Daughter; it was given twelve performances, which, in the repertory conditions of the time, meant more of a success than it would today. It was this theatre that inspired the last phase of his playwriting – a series of what he called *Chamber Plays*, on the analogy of Chamber Music. He labelled them 'Opus 1, 2, 3, and 4' and one of them he even called a sonata. This, *The Ghost Sonata*, was the only one to achieve any great success, although it is the most obscure of all his plays.

But the Strindberg Theatre soon drifted into debt and had to close – a misfortune that Strindberg naturally suspected was the work of his enemies. One good thing came out of it, however, for it was there that he met a young actress, Fanny Falkner. Though they became engaged, Fröken Falkner could not bring herself to marry this difficult old man, but she and her mother – in whose house he now took a flat, looked after him in a way that he had probably never known before, and for a time he was happy. He adored Fanny's small sisters and wrote a fairy play, *Abu Casem's Slippers*, for them. His Swedenborgian dialogues, the three *Blue Books*, were progressing, and he also became interested in semantics and wrote two treatises, one on the Swedish language and the other on the origins of the languages of the world. Three more historical plays of no great value followed, and one last 'Chamber Play', *The Black Glove*.

His sixtieth birthday in 1909 was marked by four of his plays being produced in Stockholm, while Fanny Falkner was playing *Swanwhite* in Uppsala; and at night the students sang under his windows.

In 1910 he was offered a column in a daily newspaper which became a great success and won him back nearly all the popularity that he had lost. He felt though that he had not much longer to live, and he determined to write one last play reconciling the struggle within him between heaven and earth. *The Great Highway* was not what the public had come to expect from the old firebrand, and it was given only one performance.

His devotion to children never flagged, and it was a tremendous pleasure to him that his elder daughter, Siri's child Karin, was married from his flat in 1911.

His sixty-third birthday was again an occasion for national homage. Gala performances of his plays were given, and gifts and telegrams flooded in from Europe and America. Processions with banners and torches marched below his windows proclaiming him Sweden's greatest writer, and, even though he was recovering from an attack of pneumonia, he acknowledged the cheers from his balcony, and he and Anne-Marie sprinkled flowers on the crowd.

By Easter he was dying: though an operation for cancer of the stomach had done little to relieve his continuous pain, he managed to keep up his daily newspaper article almost to the end. Four weeks before he died came news of Siri's death, and in his grief he could now admit, what he had been at such pains to deny, that she was the woman he had loved most of all.

A day or two later he wrote to his beloved Anne-Marie, now ten years old, asking her not to visit him again, as the paraphernalia of sickness was 'not a pleasant sight'; and begging her 'not to grieve for an old man who only longs to depart'. Characteristically he gave detailed orders for his funeral; he was to be buried quietly, at eight o'clock in the morning – he had always loved the dawn – in the ordinary cemetery. He died early on 14 May 1912, with the Bible clasped to his breast, murmuring 'All is atoned for'. And artists, musicians, actors, statesmen, students, and hundreds of the ordinary citizens of Stockholm followed his coffin to the grave.

THE FATHER

A TRAGEDY IN THREE ACTS

(1887)

STRINDBERG wrote this play at the time when his marriage with Siri von Essen was finally breaking up. Much of the torment of those unhappy years has gone into it; though, as always, a great deal of the suffering was bred out of Strindberg's own dark imaginings. The sinister Laura must not for a moment be taken as a portrait of Siri, who was a petite, fair, empty-headed little thing, whose vivacious charm, exercised on everyone she came in contact with, roused Strindberg's savage jealousy – even against her maid and her dog! Whatever the rights and wrongs of the matter, it was, with his persecution complex, an easy step to the conviction that she had been unfaithful.

He had already written his bitter short stories of married life, and now he returned to dramatic form, as he was always to do when he had anything that particularly clamoured for expression. Defying the accepted theatrical fashions of his day, he put the play in a single set, and with as few characters as possible.

Fatherhood had always meant a great deal to Strindberg – he had even shared, in a mystical way, in the pains of Siri's confinements. It was not surprising that, in his unstable condition, he should begin to have doubts on this very score, and to suspect that his children were not his own. As always with any intense emotion, he embodied these dark imaginings in a play.

There were two other obsessions in his mind, apart from his marital troubles, when he wrote *The Father*. The first was with the Feminists, whom he felt had been so infuriated by the two volumes of *Married* that they were continually plotting to undo him. It was only natural that a play written at this time should show women as the great enemy. The other was with the power of suggestion, of which his letters at this time were full. He had been much impressed with Shakespeare's *Othello*, and he was convinced that suggestion was a more subtle method of murder than poison or the knife.

This is one of the least obscure of Strindberg's plays; even the Captain's more inconsequential remarks seem natural, coming from his disordered mind. Here too, more than in any of the other plays, the episodes from the author's own life are carefully chosen for their aptness to the theme and his characters, and are well digested into the construction of the play.

There is little that needs explaining. At the end of Act Two, his hero throws a lighted lamp at his wife; this extraordinary scene (which is almost impossible to make credible in the theatre) might well be suspected of having come from some incident in his own life. In fact, we learn from his letters that he got the idea from England, it being, he understood, 'the habit of English husbands to throw lamps at their wives – which, considering English women, is not surprising'.

In the scene between the Captain and the Doctor in the second act, Strindberg cannot resist a little dig at Ibsen. He loathed what he called 'that famous Norwegian blue-stocking', and regarded him as his only rival. (Ibsen, on the other hand, once prophesied that Strindberg would become the greater writer of the two.)

As for other autobiographical references in the play: there is no evidence that Siri ever tampered with Strindberg's correspondence; Strindberg, however, often opened *her* letters in his efforts to trap her, so he would tend to convince himself that she had done the same to him.

Bertha's scene with the Nurse probably harks back to his own Pietist upbringing in the gloomy house in the Klara district, where the servants would terrify the children with ghost stories.

There were indeed quarrels with Siri over the education of the three children. These had become so bitter by 1886 that she began, not without cause, to suspect his sanity, and – like Laura – had called in a doctor to examine him.

Strindberg himself was born prematurely, and the thought that he was unwanted by the moth, he adored darkened his whole life.

The play was written not merely to show what an unscrupulous woman could do to a man and his reason, but also to prove, both to himself and to the world, that his own intellect was unimpaired.

THE FATHER

CHARACTERS

THE CAPTAIN
LAURA, *his wife*
BERTHA, *their daughter*
DR ÖSTERMARK
THE PASTOR
OLD MARGRET, *the nurse*
NÖJD
SVÄRD, *the orderly*

ACT ONE

[*A living-room in the* CAPTAIN*'s house. Down right is a door. There is a large round table in the centre with newspapers and magazines. To the right there is a leather sofa and another table, and in the corner, up right, a flat, wall-papered door. On the left, a sideboard with a clock, and a door to the other rooms. The walls are hung with weapons; guns and gamebags. Military greatcoats hang on hooks by the door. There is a lamp burning on the large table.*

The CAPTAIN *and the* PASTOR *are on the sofa. The* CAPTAIN *is in undress uniform, with cavalry boots and spurs. The* PASTOR *is in black, with a white neckcloth, but without his clerical collar; he is smoking a pipe.*

The CAPTAIN *rings the bell.*]

ORDERLY: You wanted something, sir?
CAPTAIN: Is Nöjd out there?
ORDERLY: Nöjd's in the kitchen, sir, waiting for orders.
CAPTAIN: In the kitchen again? Send him in here at once.

ORDERLY: Very good, sir.

[*He goes.*]

PASTOR: What's the matter now?

CAPTAIN: Oh, the rascal has been playing around with the maid again. The fellow's a thoroughly bad lot.

PASTOR: Nöjd? Didn't he do rather well earlier this year?

CAPTAIN: Yes, that's the chap. I wish you'd be kind enough to have a little talk to him. You might do him some good. I've sworn at him, I've even thrashed him, but it didn't make the slightest impression on him.

PASTOR: So now you'd like me to preach at him. What effect d'you think God's word would have on a trooper?

CAPTAIN: Well, as you know, my dear brother-in-law, it hasn't had much on me.

PASTOR: It certainly hasn't.

CAPTAIN: But – well, it might be worth trying with him. Ah, Nöjd, what have you been up to now?

NÖJD: Beg pardon, Captain, but I can't very well talk about it, not with the Pastor here.

PASTOR: There's no need to be shy with me, my boy.

CAPTAIN: You'd better make a clean breast of it – otherwise, you know what you'll get.

NÖJD: Well then, it was like this. We were having a dance at Gabriel's, you see, and Ludwig was saying –

CAPTAIN: What has Ludwig to do with it? Stick to the point.

NÖJD: Yes sir; well then, Emma said 'Let's go out to the barn'.

CAPTAIN: Oh, so I suppose it was Emma who led *you* astray?

NÖJD: Well yes, sir, in a way it was. I always say nothing ever comes of it unless the girl wants it, too.

CAPTAIN: Once and for all, are you the father of the child or not?

NÖJD: Well, how can I tell?

CAPTAIN: What do you mean? Don't you *know*?

NÖJD: No. That's a thing you can never know for certain.

CAPTAIN: Weren't you the only one, then?

NÖJD: That time, yes. But how's a man to be sure he's always been the only one?

CAPTAIN: You'd like to put the blame on Ludwig? Is that it?

NÖJD: How am I to know who's to blame?

CAPTAIN: But you told Emma that you'd marry her.

NÖJD: Oh, you always have to tell them that.

CAPTAIN [to Pastor]: This is really going too far.

PASTOR: It's the old story. Listen, Nöjd, surely you're man enough to know if you're the father.

NÖJD: Well, of course she and I . . . But you know yourself, Pastor, that nothing need come of that.

PASTOR: Look here, my lad, we're talking about *you* now. Surely you don't just mean to leave the girl with a child. I suppose you can't be forced to marry her, but you shall provide for the child, *that* you shall.

NÖJD: Yes, but Ludwig must help, too.

CAPTAIN: Then the Court'll have to decide. I've done all I can. Besides, it's not really my affair. All right, clear out.

PASTOR: Nöjd, just a minute. Er – don't you think it's rather disgraceful to leave a girl penniless like that, with a baby? Don't you think so? Well? Doesn't it strike you that that sort of behaviour's . . . well . . . a bit . . .

NÖJD: If I knew for certain that I was the father, yes; but, your Reverence, no one can ever be sure. And it's no joke slaving all your life to support another man's child. Surely you see that, Sir, and you, your Reverence.

CAPTAIN: Clear out!

NÖJD: God bless you, Captain.

CAPTAIN: And don't go back to the kitchen, you scoundrel. [NÖJD goes. The CAPTAIN turns to the PASTOR] Well, why didn't you pitch into him?

PASTOR: What do you mean? I let him have it, didn't I?

CAPTAIN: Tcha, you just sat there mumbling to yourself!

PASTOR: To tell you the truth, I didn't really know what to say.

It's hard luck on the girl, I agree, but it's hard luck on the boy too. I mean, suppose he's *not* the father. The girl can stay in the orphanage and nurse the child for four months, and then it's looked after for the rest of its life. It isn't as if that boy could help to nurse it. Afterwards, the girl can get a good place with some respectable family, but the boy's whole future might be ruined if he were dismissed from the regiment.

CAPTAIN: Upon my soul, I shouldn't like to be the Magistrate who has to judge this case. Probably the boy's not altogether innocent – we'll never know; but we do know that the girl's guilty – if you can call it guilt.

PASTOR: Yes – well, who am I to judge . . . What were we talking about, when this unfortunate business interrupted us? Bertha's confirmation, wasn't it?

CAPTAIN: Well, not so much her confirmation, as her whole education. This house is full of women who all want to bring up my daughter. My mother-in-law wants to make a spiritualist of her; Laura wants her to be an artist; the governess wants to make her a Methodist; old Margret, a Baptist; and the maids, a Salvation Army lass. It's no earthly good trying to mould a character like a piece of patchwork – especially when I, who should have most voice in her upbringing, meet with nothing but opposition. I shall have to get her away from here.

PASTOR: You certainly have too many women running your house for you!

CAPTAIN: I have, haven't I? It's like going into a cage full of tigers; if I didn't keep my red-hot irons under their noses, they'd tear me to pieces in half a minute. And you laugh, you wretch! As if it wasn't enough that I married your sister, you palm off your old stepmother on me as well.

PASTOR: But, good heavens, a man can't have a stepmother living in his house.

CAPTAIN: No, a mother-in-law – in someone else's house – suits you better!

PASTOR: Ah well, we all have our troubles in this life.

CAPTAIN: I dare say, but I have more than my share. I even have my old nurse here, treating me as if I still wore a bib. She's a dear old soul, heaven knows, but she oughtn't to be here.

PASTOR: You should keep your women-folk in order, Adolf; you let them run things far too much.

CAPTAIN: Very well then, perhaps you'd tell me just how to keep women in order?

PASTOR: Strict discipline – that's what Laura had; but, though she's my own sister, she was always a bit tiresome.

CAPTAIN: Oh, of course Laura has her faults, but they don't amount to much.

PASTOR: Come on, speak out! – I know her.

CAPTAIN: She was brought up with a lot of romantic ideas, so she finds it rather hard to adapt herself. Still, she's my wife. . . .

PASTOR: And because she's your wife, she must be perfect! No, my dear chap, she's really the one who plagues you most.

CAPTAIN: Well anyhow, the whole house is at sixes and sevens. Laura won't let Bertha go, and I can't let her stay in this madhouse.

PASTOR: Laura won't, eh? You know, I'm afraid you're in for trouble. When she was a child she used to lie on the floor like a corpse till she got her own way, then if it was some special thing she was after, as soon as she'd got it, she used to give it back! She'd say that it wasn't the *thing* she wanted so much as getting her own way.

CAPTAIN: So – she was like that even then? Hm. You know, she sometimes flies into such a rage that I'm really afraid she might be ill.

PASTOR: What is your plan for Bertha that's caused so much argument? Can't you compromise somehow?

CAPTAIN: You mustn't think I want to make her into some sort of a prodigy – nor even just another edition of myself. But I will not become a pander for my own daughter, and bring her up with no idea except marriage. You see, that would make it so hard on her if she never married after all.

On the other hand, I don't want to persuade her into taking a long course of training for some career more suited to a man, when it would all be wasted if she ever did decide to marry.

PASTOR: What is your idea, then?

CAPTAIN: I want her to be a teacher. Then, if she doesn't marry, she can always support herself — at any rate as well as those poor schoolmasters who have to provide for a family on their pay. And if she does marry, she can use her training in bringing up her own children. Don't you think I'm right?

PASTOR: Perfectly. On the other hand, hasn't she shown such a gift for painting that it would be almost a crime not to encourage it?

CAPTAIN: Not at all! I showed her efforts to a well-known artist, and he said they were only up to school-girl standard. Then, this summer, along comes a young whippersnapper who knows better, and he says she shows superb talent; so, that settles it — in Laura's mind, at any rate!

PASTOR: I suppose he'd fallen in love with the girl?

CAPTAIN: Oh, of course.

PASTOR: Then may heaven help you, my dear chap, because I can't see much help for you from any other quarter! But it's most annoying for you, and of course Laura has her supporters [indicating door] — through there.

CAPTAIN: Oh, you can be sure of that. The whole house is up in arms already, and, between ourselves, the other side's none too particular what weapons it uses.

PASTOR [rising]: Do you think I don't know?

CAPTAIN: You?

PASTOR: Of course.

CAPTAIN: But the worst of it is, it looks to me as if they're deciding Bertha's future in there out of sheer spite. They drop hints about men being made to see that women can do this, that, and the other. It's man versus woman the whole day long in this house, without a break. Oh, must you go? Do stay for supper — it won't be anything very grand, but do stay; I'm expecting the new doctor, you know. Have you seen him yet?

PASTOR: I caught a glimpse of him, on my way. He seemed a decent, reliable sort of chap.

CAPTAIN: That's good. Do you think he might be on my side?

PASTOR: Possibly. It depends how much he's lived among women.

CAPTAIN: Mm. Look, won't you stay?

PASTOR: No, thanks, my dear chap, I promised I'd be in to supper, and the old lady gets anxious if I'm late.

CAPTAIN: 'Anxious'? You mean 'angry'. All right, have it your own way. Let me help you on with your coat.

PASTOR: It's certainly turned cold tonight. Thank you. You ought to look after yourself, Adolf, you seem a bit on edge.

CAPTAIN: I? On edge?

PASTOR: Yes, are you feeling off colour?

CAPTAIN: I suppose Laura put that idea into your head? For the last twenty years she's been treating me as if I had one foot in the grave.

PASTOR: Laura? No, but — well, I don't like the look of you. Take care of yourself, that's all I say. Goodbye, old man — Oh, didn't you want to talk about the confirmation?

CAPTAIN: Not in the least. I assure you *that* will go ahead in the ordinary way; it's a matter for your professional conscience. I'm no witness to the faith, and I'm no martyr — but we've had all that out before. Good night — remember me to your family.

PASTOR: Good night, Adolf — say good night to Laura for me.

[*He goes. The* CAPTAIN *opens his desk and sits at it, doing his accounts.*]

CAPTAIN: Thirty-four — nine, forty-three — seven, eight, fifty-six —

LAURA [*coming in from the next room*]: Would you mind —

CAPTAIN: Just a moment — sixty-six, seventy-one — eighty-four, eighty-nine, ninety-two, a hundred. What is it?

LAURA: Am I interrupting?

CAPTAIN: Not at all. I suppose you want some housekeeping money?

LAURA: Yes, housekeeping money.

CAPTAIN: Leave the accounts here, and I'll go over them.

LAURA: Accounts?

CAPTAIN: Yes.

LAURA: Do I have to keep accounts, now?

CAPTAIN: Of course you must keep accounts. Things are in a bad way with us, and if I should go bankrupt, I must be able to produce accounts, or they could accuse me of negligence.

LAURA: It's not *my* fault if things are in a bad way.

CAPTAIN: Then the accounts would confirm that.

LAURA: I can't help it if the lodger didn't pay.

CAPTAIN: Who was so enthusiastic about the man? You. Why do you recommend such a – what shall I call him – such a ne'er-do-well?

LAURA: Why did you take in such a ne'er-do-well?

CAPTAIN: Because I wasn't allowed to eat or sleep or work in peace until you'd got him in here. You wanted him because your brother wanted to get rid of him; your mother wanted him because I *didn't*. The governess wanted him because he was a Pietist; and old Margret, because she'd known his grandmother ever since she was a baby. That's why I took him in – because if I hadn't, I should be in the lunatic asylum by now, or in the family vault. However, here's the housekeeping money, and your allowance. You can give me the accounts later.

LAURA [*dropping a curtsy*]: Thank you so much! And do *you* keep an account of what you spend – apart from the housekeeping?

CAPTAIN: That's nothing to do with you.

LAURA: True – just as my child's education is nothing to do with me. Did my lords come to any decision at this evening's session?

CAPTAIN: I'd made up my mind already, I merely wished to inform the only friend I and my household have in common.

Bertha is to live in town; she'll leave in a fortnight's time.

LAURA: And where is she to live – if I'm allowed to ask?

CAPTAIN: With the lawyer, Mr Sävberg.

LAURA: That Freethinker!

CAPTAIN: As the law stands, children must be brought up in their father's faith.

LAURA: And the mother has no say in the matter?

CAPTAIN: None whatever. By law she surrenders all her rights and possessions to her husband, and in return he must support her and her children.

LAURA: So she has no rights over her own child?

CAPTAIN: None whatever. Once you've sold your goods, you can't expect to have them back *and* keep the money.

LAURA: But if the father and the mother agree on a compromise . . .

CAPTAIN: How could they? I want her to live in the town, you want her to live at home. Mathematically, a compromise would mean that she stayed at the railway station – half-way between the two. It's one of those knots that there's no untying, you see.

LAURA: Then it must be cut! What was Nöjd doing here?

CAPTAIN: That's an official and confidential matter –

LAURA: – that the whole kitchen knows about.

CAPTAIN: Good – then you know it too.

LAURA: Yes, I know it.

CAPTAIN: And you've passed judgement already?

LAURA: The law's perfectly clear.

CAPTAIN: The law can't say who is the child's father.

LAURA: You can usually tell.

CAPTAIN: They say that's something you can never be sure of.

LAURA: How extraordinary! You can't be sure who a child's father is?

CAPTAIN: So they say.

LAURA: Extraordinary. Then how is it that the father has such rights over a woman's children?

CAPTAIN: He has the rights simply because he takes on the responsibilities – or has them forced on him. In marriage, naturally there's no doubt about the paternity.

LAURA: No doubt?

CAPTAIN: I should hope not.

LAURA: Suppose the wife were unfaithful?

CAPTAIN: That question doesn't arise in this case. Is there anything else you want to ask?

LAURA: No, nothing.

CAPTAIN: Then I shall go up to my room. Let me know when the Doctor comes, please.

[*He shuts the desk and gets up.*]

LAURA: Very well.

CAPTAIN [*as he goes through the private door to the right*]: The moment he arrives, please. Naturally I don't want to seem discourteous to him.

[*He goes.*]

LAURA: Naturally.

[*Left alone, she looks at the banknotes in her hand. Her* MOTHER *is heard calling, off.*]

MOTHER: Laura!

LAURA: Yes?

MOTHER: Is my tea ready?

LAURA [*at the doorway to the inner rooms*]: It's just coming.

[*She goes towards the hall door, as the* ORDERLY *opens it and announces 'Dr Östermark'.*]

DOCTOR: Good evening, madam.

LAURA [*going to him and giving him her hand*]: Come in, Doctor, we're delighted to see you. The Captain is out, but he should be back at any moment.

DOCTOR: I'm sorry to be so late, but I've had some patients to see already.

LAURA: Please sit down, won't you?

DOCTOR: Thank you, madam.

LAURA: Yes, there's a lot of illness about just now, but I'm sure you'll manage. For people like us, living in a lonely country district, it means so much to have a doctor who takes an interest in his patients; and I've heard so many nice things about you, Doctor, that I'm sure we shall get on well together.

DOCTOR: That's very kind of you, madam; I hope though, for your sake, that I shall not need to make too many *professional* calls. I should think your family is pretty healthy on the whole, so –

LAURA: Yes, we've been lucky enough to escape anything serious; still, things aren't quite as they should be.

DOCTOR: Oh?

LAURA: No, I'm afraid they're not so good as we could wish.

DOCTOR: Really? I don't like to hear that.

LAURA: There are things in family life that one is in honour bound to keep from the world, out of self-respect. . . .

DOCTOR: But not from one's doctor.

LAURA: That is why I feel I should tell you the whole truth – however painful – from the start.

DOCTOR: Hadn't it better wait till I've had the pleasure of meeting the Captain?

LAURA: No. You must hear what I have to say before you see him.

DOCTOR: It concerns him, then?

LAURA: Yes – my poor, dear husband.

DOCTOR: I'm very sorry to hear this, madam. I assure you, you have all my sympathy.

LAURA [*taking out her handkerchief*]: My husband's mind is going. Now you know it all; you'll be able to judge for yourself when you see him.

DOCTOR: I can't believe it. The Captain's papers on mineralogy are masterly; I've been most impressed when I've read them, and they've always seemed to show a particularly fine and orderly mind.

LAURA: Really? Well, I shall be delighted if we, who are nearest to him, should all be proved wrong.

DOCTOR: Tell me more about him. Of course it is possible that his mind is affected in other ways.

LAURA: That's what we're afraid of, too. You see, he sometimes has the most extraordinary ideas. Of course that's not unusual with brilliant scholars – if only it didn't threaten his whole family's welfare. For instance, he has a mania for buying all sorts of things.

DOCTOR: That's significant. What does he buy?

LAURA: Whole crates of books that he never reads.

DOCTOR: Well, there's nothing very odd in a scholar buying books.

LAURA: Don't you believe what I'm telling you?

DOCTOR: I'm quite sure, madam, that *you* believe what you're telling me.

LAURA: Then is it reasonable for a man to see through a microscope what's happening on another planet?

DOCTOR: Does he say that he can do that?

LAURA: That's what he says.

DOCTOR: Through a microscope?

LAURA: A microscope, yes.

DOCTOR: That's significant, if it's true.

LAURA: If it's true? Then you don't believe me, Doctor. And I've been letting you into our family secret. . . .

DOCTOR: My dear lady, I'm honoured that you should confide in me, but as a doctor, I must examine and investigate for myself before I make my diagnosis. Does the Captain show any symptoms of sudden moodiness – is he very changeable?

LAURA: Changeable? We've been married for twenty years now, and he's never yet made a decision without changing his mind afterwards.

DOCTOR: Is he obstinate?

LAURA: He always insists on having his own way, but the moment he gets it, he loses interest, and asks me to decide for him.

DOCTOR: That's significant; it needs very careful watching.

You see, madam, the will is the backbone of the mind; if it is affected, the whole mind collapses.

LAURA: Heaven knows I've had to bring myself to fall in with his wishes, all through these long, trying years. Oh, if you only knew what I've had to go through, living with him – if you only knew!

DOCTOR: Madam, I'm deeply moved by your misfortune, and I promise you that I'll see what can be done. I sympathize with all my heart, and I hope you will rely on me absolutely. But in view of what you've told me, there is one thing I must impress on you. Avoid bringing up any topic that is likely to affect the patient strongly. Ideas like that can develop rapidly in an unstable mind, and may easily turn to obsessions or monomania. Do you understand?

LAURA: You mean, avoid rousing his suspicions?

DOCTOR: Exactly – these patients can be made to believe anything, because they are so very receptive.

LAURA: Ah! I understand. Yes – yes. [*A bell rings, inside.*] Excuse me, my mother wants me for something. I shan't be a moment – Ah, here is Adolf.

[*The* CAPTAIN *enters by the private door.*]

CAPTAIN: Oh, you're here already, Doctor. We're very glad to see you.

DOCTOR: My dear Captain, I'm delighted to meet such a distinguished man of science.

CAPTAIN: Oh, please! My military duties leave me very little time for intensive research. Still I really believe I'm on the verge of a discovery.

DOCTOR: Oh?

CAPTAIN: You see, I've subjected meteoric stones to spectrum analysis, and I've found *coal* – a sign of organic life! What do you say to that?

DOCTOR: And can you see that through a microscope?

CAPTAIN: Good heavens, no – through a spectroscope.

DOCTOR: A spectroscope. Oh, of course. So you'll soon be

able to tell us what's happening on Jupiter.

CAPTAIN: Not what is happening, but what *has* happened. If only those wretched booksellers in Paris would send me the books! I believe all the booksellers in the world are in league against me! Would you believe it, for the last two months, not one of them has acknowledged my orders. I've written and even sent abusive telegrams! It makes me mad – I can't think what it all means.

DOCTOR: Oh, it's just ordinary carelessness; you shouldn't let it upset you so.

CAPTAIN: Yes, but the devil of it is that I shan't get my treatise finished in time, and I know they're working along the same lines in Berlin. Still, that isn't what we were going to talk about; how about you? If you'd care to stay here, there's a little flat in the annexe, or would you rather have the old doctor's quarters?

DOCTOR: Just as you like.

CAPTAIN: No, it's as *you* like. You say.

DOCTOR: You must decide, Captain.

CAPTAIN: No, I'm not going to decide; you must say which you'd prefer – it makes no difference to me – none whatever.

DOCTOR: Well, I can't really decide –

CAPTAIN: For God's sake, man, say what you want! I have no preference, no opinion, no wishes in the matter. Are you such a weakling that you don't know your own mind? Tell me, or I shall lose my temper.

DOCTOR: Well, if it's up to me, I should like to live here.

CAPTAIN: Thank you; that's better. Do forgive me, Doctor, but nothing annoys me more than to hear people say 'it's all the same to me'! [*He rings the bell, and the* NURSE *comes in.*] Ah, there you are, Margret. Look, my dear, do you know if the annexe is ready for the Doctor?

NURSE: Yes, Captain.

CAPTAIN: Good. Then I won't keep you any longer, Doctor;

you must be tired. Goodbye, and I hope I shall see you again in the morning.

DOCTOR: Good night, Captain.

CAPTAIN: I expect that my wife has told you a little about us, so you'll have some idea how the land lies.

DOCTOR: Yes, your charming wife did give me one or two hints about things that a stranger ought to know. Good night, Captain.

[*He goes.*]

CAPTAIN [*to Nurse*]: What do you want, my dear? Is anything the matter?

NURSE: Now, Master Adolf, just you listen to me.

CAPTAIN: Yes, old Margret – talk away. You're the only one I can listen to without getting in a rage.

NURSE: Now, just listen, Mr Adolf – don't you think you ought to meet the mistress half-way in all this bother over the child? Think how a mother feels –

CAPTAIN: Think how a father feels, Margret.

NURSE: Now, now, now! A father has other things to think of, but a mother has only her child.

CAPTAIN: Exactly, old lady! She has only one anxiety, while I have three – as well as all hers. Don't you think I should have been something more in the world than a poor soldier, if I hadn't had her and her child?

NURSE: Yes, but that isn't what I meant.

CAPTAIN: No, I'm sure it wasn't; you wanted me to admit that I'm in the wrong.

NURSE: Now, Mr Adolf, you believe I want to help, don't you?

CAPTAIN: Yes, my dear, I do, but you don't know what is best for me. You see, it's not enough for me just to have given the child *life*, I want to give her my intellect, too.

NURSE: Oh, I don't understand anything about that. But I do think you ought to be able to agree.

CAPTAIN: You're not my friend, Margret.

NURSE: Me? Goodness, Mr Adolf, how can you say such a

thing? Do you think I can forget how you were my baby when you were little?

CAPTAIN: Do you imagine I've forgotten it, dear? You've been like a mother to me. Up to now, you've always stood by me when they were all against me; but now, when I really need you, you desert me and go over to the enemy.

NURSE: The enemy?

CAPTAIN: Yes, the enemy! You know well enough how things stand in this house. You've seen it all from the very beginning.

NURSE: Yes, I've seen, all right. But, my goodness, why must two people plague the life out of each other? Two people who are so good and kind to everyone else. The mistress is never like that with me – or with anyone else –

CAPTAIN: Yes, I know – only with me. Listen to me, Margret: if you desert me now, you'd be doing me a great wrong. You see they're plotting against me now – and that Doctor's no friend of mine.

NURSE: Now then, Mr Adolf, you always think the worst of everyone. It's because you haven't the true Faith, you see, that's what it is.

CAPTAIN: And you and the Baptists have found the only real faith. Happy people!

NURSE: Anyway, I'm not as unhappy as you, Mr Adolf. Humble your heart, and you'll see how God will make you happy, and loving towards your neighbour.

CAPTAIN: It's wonderful how, the moment you talk about God and love, your voice becomes hard, and your eyes fill with hatred. No, Margret, you certainly haven't the true faith.

NURSE: Yes, it's your learning makes you proud and hard, but it won't help you much in the hour of tribulation!

CAPTAIN: You talk very proudly for a humble heart! I know how little learning means to people like you.

NURSE: You ought to be ashamed of yourself. But, in spite of everything, old Margret loves her great big boy best; and when he's in trouble, he'll come back to her again, like a good little child.

CAPTAIN: I'm sorry, Margret; but, believe me, you're the only one in this house who's on my side. I want you to help me, because I feel that something's going to happen here – I don't know what, but whatever it is, it'll be evil. [*Screams from off-stage.*] What's that? Who screamed?

[BERTHA *comes in.*]

BERTHA: Help! Papa, papa! Save me!

CAPTAIN: What's the matter, darling? Tell me.

BERTHA: Help me! She'll hurt me. I know she will.

CAPTAIN: Who's going to hurt you? Tell me – quickly.

BERTHA: Grandmama! It was my fault, though; I played a trick on her.

CAPTAIN: Go on.

BERTHA: All right, but you mustn't say anything. You won't, will you? Please!

CAPTAIN: Suppose you tell me what it is.

[*Nurse goes.*]

BERTHA: Well, in the evenings, she likes to turn the lamp down, and then I have to sit at the table and hold a pen over a sheet of paper. And then she commands the spirits to write.

CAPTAIN: Good heavens! Why didn't you tell me?

BERTHA: I'm sorry, but I didn't dare. Grandmama says the spirits take their revenge if anyone talks about them. And the the pen writes but I don't know if it's me doing it. Sometimes it works beautifully, but sometimes it won't go at all. When I'm tired, it doesn't, but I have to make *something* come. This evening I thought I was doing it beautifully, but Grandmama said it was all out of Stagnelius, and that I'd been cheating her, and she got terrible angry.

CAPTAIN: Do you believe that there are such things as spirits?

BERTHA: I don't know.

CAPTAIN: Well, I know there aren't.

BERTHA: But Grandmama says you don't understand, and she

says you have things that are far worse – things that can see to other planets.

CAPTAIN: Does she? Does she indeed? What else does she say?

BERTHA: She says you can't do magic.

CAPTAIN: I've never said I could. Do you know what meteors are? They're stones that fall from other heavenly bodies. What I do is to examine them, and say whether they're made of the same elements as our earth. That's all I can see.

BERTHA: But Grandmama says there are things that she can see and you can't.

CAPTAIN: Then I tell you she's lying.

BERTHA: Grandmama doesn't tell lies.

CAPTAIN: Why not?

BERTHA: Because then Mama tells lies too.

CAPTAIN: Ah.

BERTHA: If you say that Mama tells lies, then I'll never believe you again.

CAPTAIN: I didn't say so. That's why you must believe me when I tell you that for your own good, for the sake of your whole future, you must leave this house. Will you do that? Would you like to go to the town and learn something useful?

BERTHA: Oh yes! I'd love to go to the town – anywhere, to get away from here. So long as I can see you sometimes – often. Oh, it's so horrid and dull in there all the time – just like a winter night ; but when you come, Papa, it's like the spring morning when they take down the double windows.

CAPTAIN: My dear, darling child!

BERTHA: But Papa, you must be kind to Mama, you know. She does cry such a lot.

CAPTAIN: Ah. So you want to go and live in the town?

BERTHA: Oh yes, please!

CAPTAIN: But suppose Mama doesn't want you to.

BERTHA: Oh, she must.

CAPTAIN: But suppose she doesn't?

BERTHA: Oh well then I don't know what will happen. But she must – she simply must!

CAPTAIN: Will you ask her?

BERTHA: No, you must ask her – very nicely. She never takes any notice of me.

CAPTAIN: Hm. Well, suppose you want it and I want it, but she doesn't want it – what shall we do then?

BERTHA: Oh then everything'll be tiresome again. Why can't you two –

LAURA [coming in]: Ah, Bertha's in here! Then perhaps we can hear what *she* thinks, since it's her future that's to be decided.

CAPTAIN: The child can hardly have any considered opinion about how a young girl's life may develop. We, on the other hand, have seen plenty of girls grow up, so it's easier for us to arrive at some sort of an answer.

LAURA: But since we have different ideas, surely Bertha might have the casting vote.

CAPTAIN: No, I'll have no one – woman or child – encroaching on my rights. Leave us, Bertha.

[BERTHA goes.]

LAURA: You were afraid to let her speak, because you thought she'd be on my side.

CAPTAIN: I know that what she wants is to leave home, but I also know that you have the power to make her change her mind when you like.

LAURA: Oh, am I as powerful as that?

CAPTAIN: Yes, when it comes to getting your own way you have the power of the devil, but so has everyone who's unscrupulous enough. For example, how did you get rid of Dr Nordling, and how did you get the new man here?

LAURA: Well? How did I?

CAPTAIN: You insulted Nordling till he left; and then you got your brother to scrape up votes for this man.

LAURA: Well, that was very simple, and quite legitimate. So Bertha's to go away?

CAPTAIN: Yes, she's to leave in a fortnight's time.

LAURA: Is that your last word?

CAPTAIN: Yes.

LAURA: Have you told Bertha?

CAPTAIN: Yes.

LAURA: Then I must try to stop it.

CAPTAIN: You can't.

LAURA: Can't I? Do you really think that a mother is going to send her child among wicked people who'll say that all her mother has taught her is stupid? Why, the daughter would despise her for the rest of her life.

CAPTAIN: Do *you* think a father would let ignorant and conceited women teach his daughter that he is a charlatan?

LAURA: It's less important to a father.

CAPTAIN: Oh? Why?

LAURA: Because a mother's nearer to the child – since it's been discovered that no one can tell for certain who is a child's father.

CAPTAIN: What has that to do with it?

LAURA: Simply that you don't know that you are Bertha's father.

CAPTAIN: Of course I know!

LAURA: 'No one can tell', so you certainly can't.

CAPTAIN: Is this a joke?

LAURA: No, I'm simply applying your own doctrine. Besides, how do you know that I haven't been unfaithful to you?

CAPTAIN: I can believe a lot about you, but not that. Nor do I believe that you'd talk about it if it were true.

LAURA: Suppose I were ready to put up with anything, to lose my home and my good name, for the sake of keeping my child and bringing her up. Suppose I was telling the truth just now when I said Bertha was my child and not yours. Suppose –

CAPTAIN: Stop!

LAURA: Suppose it were true, you'd have no more rights.

CAPTAIN: If you could prove that I were not the father.

LAURA: That wouldn't be difficult. Would you like me to?

CAPTAIN: Stop it!

LAURA: You see, I should only need to give the name of the real father, with details of the time and place; for instance – when was Bertha born? We'd been married three years –

CAPTAIN: Stop this, or –

LAURA: Or what? All right then, we'll stop. But think very carefully before you decide to do anything. Above all, don't make yourself look ridiculous.

CAPTAIN: I think this is all very unfortunate.

LAURA: That makes you even more ridiculous.

CAPTAIN: But not you?

LAURA: No, we women manage these things more cleverly.

CAPTAIN: That's why we can't fight you.

LAURA: Then why get involved in fights with a superior enemy?

CAPTAIN: Superior?

LAURA: Yes. It's odd, but I've never been able to look at a man without feeling that I'm his superior.

CAPTAIN: Well, one day you'll meet your match – and you'll never forget it.

LAURA: That will be interesting.

NURSE [coming in]: Supper's ready. Won't you please come out and have it.

LAURA: Thank you. [The CAPTAIN stays behind, sitting in the armchair by the sofa-table.] Are you coming to supper?

CAPTAIN: No, thank you, I don't want any.

LAURA: Oh? Is something the matter?

CAPTAIN: No, I'm not hungry.

LAURA: Come along, or they'll be . . . asking tiresome questions. Don't be difficult. All right, if you won't, then stay where you are.

[She goes.]

NURSE: Oh, Mr Adolf, what is all this about?

CAPTAIN: I don't know. Can you explain how you women manage to treat a grown man as if he were a child?

NURSE: I don't understand it, but I suppose it's because you are all women's children, every one of you, great or small . . .

CAPTAIN: While no woman is born of *man*. But then I *am* Bertha's father. Tell me, Margret, you do believe that, don't you?

NURSE: Lord, what a baby you are! Of course you're the father of your own child. Come and have supper, now, and don't sit there sulking. There, there; come along now!

CAPTAIN [*getting up*]: Get out of here, woman! Go to hell, you witches! [*He goes to inner door.*] Svärd! Svärd!

ORDERLY [*coming in*]: Yes, sir?

CAPTAIN: Have the fast sleigh harnessed at once.

NURSE: Captain, only listen —

CAPTAIN: Get out, woman — at once.

NURSE: Lord preserve us, what's going to happen now?

CAPTAIN [*putting on his cap, and preparing to go out*]: Don't expect me back before midnight!

[*He goes.*]

NURSE: God help us! What will be the end of this?

CURTAIN

ACT TWO

[The scene is the same as in the previous Act. It is night, and the lamp on the table is alight.]

DOCTOR: From what I could gather as we talked, I'm not entirely convinced about the case. In the first place, you made a mistake when you said he arrived at his extraordinary conclusions about other heavenly bodies by means of a microscope. Now that I find that it was a spectroscope, he's not only cleared of any suspicion of mental disorder, but he has actually made a great contribution to science.

LAURA: Yes, but I never said that!

DOCTOR: Madam, I made notes of our conversation, and I remember questioning you on that particular point, because I thought I must have misheard you. One has to be careful about making an accusation that could lead to a man being certified.

LAURA: Certified?

DOCTOR: Yes; you know, of course, that an insane person loses his civil and family rights.

LAURA: No, I didn't know that.

DOCTOR: There's one other point that strikes me as suspicious. He spoke about his correspondence with the booksellers going unanswered. May I ask if – out of misplaced kindness – *you* intercepted it?

LAURA: Yes, I did. It was my duty to look after the interests of the house; I couldn't stand idly by and let him ruin us all.

DOCTOR: Forgive my saying so, but I don't think you can have considered the consequences of such a step. If he were to discover that you've been secretly meddling in his affairs, he would have cause for his suspicions, and then they'd grow like an avalanche. Moreover by your action you have thwarted his will, and increased his irritability. You yourself must have found how infuriating it can be when one's dearest wishes are thwarted and one's will obstructed.

LAURA: As if I didn't know that.

DOCTOR: Then think how it must have affected him.

LAURA [*getting up*]: It's midnight, and he's not back yet. I'm afraid something terrible may have happened.

DOCTOR: Madam, tell me what took place this evening after I left? I must know everything.

LAURA: His mind wandered, and he had the most extraordinary fancy. Just imagine, he had an idea that he wasn't the father of his own child.

DOCTOR: That was odd. What put that into his head?

LAURA: I don't know at all, unless it was that he had to interview one of the men on some question of a maintenance order, and when I took the girl's part, he became excited and said that no one could tell who was the father of a child. Heaven knows I did all I could to calm him, but I'm beginning to think that he's beyond help.

[*She cries.*]

DOCTOR: But things can't go on like this; something must be done, and without arousing his suspicions. Tell me, has the Captain ever had these fancies before?

LAURA: Six years ago we had much the same trouble, and then he actually admitted, in his own letter to the doctor, that he was afraid his mind was going.

DOCTOR: Yes, yes, yes, a case like this is deep-rooted, and what with the sanctity of family life, and so forth, I can't probe too deeply; I must confine myself to the obvious symptoms. What's done can't be undone, unfortunately – yet the treatment must have some relation to what's gone before. Where do you think he is now?

LAURA: I've no idea, he has such wild fancies nowadays.

DOCTOR: Would you like me to stay till he comes back? To avoid suspicion I could say that your mother wasn't well and that I'd come to see her.

LAURA: Yes, that would do splendidly. Don't leave us, Doctor;

if only you knew how anxious I am. But wouldn't it be better to tell him outright what you think of his condition?

DOCTOR: One never does that with a mental patient, unless he brings up the subject himself, and then only in exceptional cases. It depends entirely on what course the illness takes. But we mustn't sit here; perhaps it would look more natural if I went into the next room.

LAURA: Yes, that would be better, then Margret can sit here. She always waits for him when he's out; besides, she's the only one who has any influence over him. [*She goes to the door on the left.*] Margret! Margret!

NURSE: Did you want something, ma'am? Is the master back?

LAURA: No, but I want you to sit here and wait for him; and when he comes, you're to tell him that my mother's ill, and that's why the doctor's here.

NURSE: Yes, yes, I'll see that everything's all right.

LAURA [*opening the door to the inner rooms*]: Will you come in here, Doctor?

DOCTOR: Thank you, madam.

[*The* NURSE *sits at the table and takes up a hymnbook and her spectacles.*]

NURSE: Yes, yes . . . [*She reads, half aloud:*]

> 'A pitiful and wretched thing
> Is life, that swiftly passes by.
> Death's angel o'er us spreads his wing
> And through the world resounds his cry:
> "All must perish, all is vain!"'

Ah yes!

> 'All that upon this earth draws breath
> To earth must fall beneath his doom,
> Sorrow alone escapes our death,
> To carve upon the gaping tomb:
> "All must perish, all is vain!"'

Yes indeed –

[BERTHA *comes in with a coffee-pot and a piece of needlework. She speaks softly:*]

BERTHA: Margret, may I sit with you? It's so lonely up there.

NURSE: Why, bless my soul, Bertha, aren't you in bed yet?

BERTHA: You see, I want to finish Papa's Christmas present. And I've brought something you'll like, too.

NURSE: Yes, but, my dear, this will never do. It's gone twelve o'clock, and you've got to be up in the morning.

BERTHA: What does it matter? I daren't stay up there all alone, I think it's haunted.

NURSE: There now, what did I say? You mark my words, there's a curse on this house. What did you hear, Bertha?

BERTHA: Well, actually, I heard someone singing up in the attic.

NURSE: In the attic? At this time of night?

BERTHA: Yes, it was such a sad song, the saddest song I've ever heard. And it seemed as if it came from the box-room – you know, on the left, where the cradle stands.

NURSE: Oh dear, oh dear! And such a fearful night too, I'm sure the chimneys'll blow down:

> 'Ah, what is our life below?
> Pain and sorrow, grief and woe.
> Even when it seemed most fair,
> Naught but agony was there.'

Yes, dear child, God send us a happy Christmas.

BERTHA: Margret, is it true that Papa's ill?

NURSE: Yes, he really is.

BERTHA: Then we shan't be able to keep Christmas Eve. But if he's ill, how can he be up?

NURSE: You see, child, with his kind of illness he doesn't have to go to bed. Ssh – there's someone out in the hall. Go to bed now – and take the coffee-pot away, or the master'll be angry.

BERTHA [taking the tray out]: Good night, Margret.

NURSE: Good night, child – and God bless you.

[The CAPTAIN enters, removing his greatcoat.]

CAPTAIN: Are you still up? Go to bed.

NURSE: I was only waiting till – [*The* CAPTAIN *lights a candle, opens his desk and, sitting at it, takes letters and newspapers out of his pocket.*] Mr Adolf.

CAPTAIN: What do you want?

NURSE: The old lady's ill, and the doctor's here.

CAPTAIN: Is it serious?

NURSE: No I don't think so – just a cold.

CAPTAIN [*getting up*]: Margret, who was the father of your child?

NURSE: Oh, I've told you time and time again: it was that scamp Johansson..

CAPTAIN: Are you sure it was he?

NURSE: You're talking like a child! Of course I'm sure, seeing he was the only one.

CAPTAIN: But was *he* sure he was the only one? No, he couldn't be, even though *you* were sure. That's the difference, you see.

NURSE: I don't see any difference.

CAPTAIN: No, you can't see it, but the difference is there all the same. [*He looks through a photograph album on the table.*] Do you think Bertha's like me?

[*He looks at a picture in the album.*]

NURSE: Why yes – you're as like as two peas.

CAPTAIN: Did Johansson admit that he was the father?

NURSE: Well, he had to!

CAPTAIN: How terrible. Here's the doctor. [*The* DOCTOR *comes in.*] Good evening doctor. How's my mother-in-law?

DOCTOR: Oh, nothing serious – only a slight sprain in the left ankle.

CAPTAIN: I thought Margret said it was a cold. There seems to be quite a difference of opinion about the case. Go to bed, Margret. [*The* NURSE *goes. Pause.*] Do sit down, doctor.

DOCTOR [*sitting*]: Thanks.

CAPTAIN: Is it true that you get striped foals if you cross a zebra with a mare?

DOCTOR [*surprised*]: Perfectly true.

CAPTAIN: Is it true that further foals may also be striped, even if the next sire is a stallion?

DOCTOR: Yes, that's true, too.

CAPTAIN: So that, under certain conditions, a stallion can sire striped foals – and vice versa?

DOCTOR: So it seems, yes.

CAPTAIN: Therefore a child's likeness to the father means nothing?

DOCTOR: Well –

CAPTAIN: That is to say, paternity cannot be proved.

DOCTOR: Hm – well –

CAPTAIN: You are a widower? And you've had children?

DOCTOR: Ye-es.

CAPTAIN: Didn't being a father sometimes make you feel ridiculous? I know of nothing more absurd than seeing a father lead his child through the street, or hearing a father talk about 'my children'. He ought to say 'my wife's children'! Didn't you ever realize what a false position you were in? Weren't you ever afflicted with doubts . . . I won't say suspicions, for, as a gentleman, I assume that your wife was above suspicion.

DOCTOR: No, as a matter of fact, I never was. And anyhow, Captain, wasn't it Goethe who said 'A man must take his children on trust'?

CAPTAIN: On trust when it concerns a woman? That's dangerous!

DOCTOR: Ah, there's more than one kind of woman, you know.

CAPTAIN: The latest researches have established that there is only *one* kind. When I was young, I was strong and – if I may say so – good-looking. I can call to mind just two brief incidents that, when I came to think of them, roused my suspicions. I was once on board a steamer, sitting with some friends in the saloon, when in came the young stewardess, in tears. She sat down and told us that her sweetheart had been drowned. We sympathized with her, and I ordered champagne. After the second glass, I touched her foot; after the fourth, her knee, and before morning, I had consoled her.

DOCTOR: One swallow doesn't make a summer.

CAPTAIN: Now for the other – and that was a real summer swallow. I was at Lysenkil. There was a young married woman staying there with her children, but her husband was in town. She was a woman of the strictest principles, and very devout; she preached morality to me, and was completely virtuous – or so I thought. I lent her one or two books, and when she went away, surprisingly enough, she returned them. Three months later, in one of those very books, I came across a visiting card, bearing a pretty obvious hint. Oh, it was perfectly innocent – as innocent, that is, as an indication of love can be, from a married woman to a strange man who has never made any advances to her. So the moral is this: don't trust them too much.

DOCTOR: Nor too little either!

CAPTAIN: No, enough and no more. But listen to this, doctor; unconsciously that woman was so despicable that she went and told her husband that she was in love with me. That's what's so dangerous – that their innate dishonesty is quite unconscious. That's an extenuating circumstance, but it doesn't alter my judgement, even if it mitigates it.

DOCTOR: Captain, you should be careful not to let your thoughts take an unhealthy turn.

CAPTAIN: You shouldn't use the word 'unhealthy'. Remember all boilers burst when their pressure-gauge reaches 100, but that hundred mark varies with different boilers, if you see what I mean. However, you're here to watch me. If I weren't a man, I should have the right to make accusations – or complaints, as they're so cleverly called, and perhaps I should be able to give you the full diagnosis and, what is more, the case history. But since I have the misfortune to be a man, I can only do like the Romans, and fold my arms over my chest and hold my breath till I die. Good night.

DOCTOR: Captain, if you are ill, it wouldn't stain your honour as a man to tell me the whole story. In fact I *ought* to hear the other side.

CAPTAIN: I should have thought that, having heard one side, you've had quite enough of it.

DOCTOR: Not at all, Captain. You know, when I heard Mrs Alving eulogizing her dead husband, I thought to myself 'what a confounded shame the fellow's dead'.

CAPTAIN: Do you think he would have spoken if he'd been alive? And do you suppose that if any dead husband were to come to life, he'd be believed? Good night, doctor. As you see, I'm quite calm, so you can safely go to bed!

DOCTOR: Good night, then, Captain. There's nothing more that I can do in this case.

CAPTAIN: Are we enemies?

DOCTOR: Far from it. The pity is that we can't be friends. Good night.

[*He goes. The* CAPTAIN *sees the* DOCTOR *to the far door, then goes to the door on the left, and opens it a little.*]

CAPTAIN: Come in, then we can talk. I heard you out there listening. [LAURA *comes in, shamefacedly; the* CAPTAIN *sits at his desk.*] It's late, but we must thrash things out. Sit down. [*Pause.*] I've been to the post-office this evening to collect the letters. From them it appears that you've been intercepting both my incoming and outgoing mail. The consequence is that the loss of time has practically ruined the results that I'd expected from my work.

LAURA: That was an act of kindness on my part; you were neglecting your duties for this other work.

CAPTAIN: It was certainly no act of kindness, since you knew perfectly well that one day this work will bring me far more honour than my military duties; but you particularly don't want me to win any honour, since it would emphasize your insignificance. That's why I've now intercepted some letters addressed to you.

LAURA: How noble of you!

CAPTAIN: Ah, I see you have a high opinion of me, as they say. From these letters, it appears that for some time now you've been setting my former friends against me by spreading a rumour about my sanity. What's more, your efforts have been successful, since there's hardly anyone, from the Colonel to the cook, who believes me sane. Now, the truth about my illness is this: my reason is unaffected as you know, since I can carry out both my duties as a soldier and my obligations as a father; I have my emotions pretty well under control, so long as my will remains more or less intact – though you've gnawed and gnawed at it so that soon it will slip its cogs and then the whole works will whirr to a standstill. I shall not appeal to your feelings, because you have none – I appeal to your own interests.

LAURA: Go on.

CAPTAIN: Your behaviour has succeeded in arousing my suspicions so much, that soon my reason will be clouded and my mind will begin to wander. That means the onset of the madness that you have been waiting for, and that may come at any time. That brings you to the question of whether it's more to your advantage that I should be sane or insane. Think it over. If I go down, I shall have to leave the Service, and where will you be then? If I die my life insurance will come to you. But if I take my own life, you will get nothing. So it's to your advantage that I should live out my life.

LAURA: Is this a trap?

CAPTAIN: Certainly. It rests with you whether you avoid it, or put your head in.

LAURA: You say that you'll kill yourself. You'll never do that.

CAPTAIN: Are you sure? Do you think a man can live when there's nothing and no one to live for?

LAURA: Then you surrender?

CAPTAIN: No, I offer you peace.

LAURA: Under what conditions?

CAPTAIN: That I keep my reason. Free me from my suspicions and I'll give up the fight.

LAURA: What suspicions?

CAPTAIN: About Bertha's parentage.

LAURA: Are there any doubts about that?

CAPTAIN: There are for me, and it's you who have raised them.

LAURA: I?

CAPTAIN: Yes, you have poured them into my ear like drops of henbane, and circumstances have made them grow. Free me from the uncertainty – tell me outright 'This is the truth' – and I will forgive you in advance.

LAURA: I can hardly plead guilty to a crime that I've not committed.

CAPTAIN: How can it matter to you, when you can be quite sure that I shall never divulge it. Do you think a man would go and trumpet his own shame abroad.

LAURA: If I said that it's not true, you wouldn't be convinced, but if I said it is, that would convince you. In fact, you want it to be true?

CAPTAIN: Yes, oddly enough – probably because the former case can't be proved, while the latter can.

LAURA: Have you any grounds for your suspicions?

CAPTAIN: Yes and no.

LAURA: I believe you want to prove me guilty so that you can get rid of me and then have full control over the child. But I'm not falling into that trap.

CAPTAIN: If I were convinced that you were guilty, do you imagine I would take on another man's child?

LAURA: No, I'm quite sure you wouldn't; that's how I know you were lying just now when you said that I was forgiven in advance.

CAPTAIN [getting up]: Laura, don't destroy me and my reason! You don't understand what I'm saying. If the child is not mine, then I have no control over her, nor do I desire any. That is just what you want, isn't it? But perhaps you want something else as well: you want to have power over the child, yet still have me to support you.

LAURA: Yes, power. What has all this life and death struggle been about except power?

CAPTAIN: For me, since I don't believe in a life to come, my child was my after-life. She was my idea of immortality – perhaps the only one that has any foundation in reality. Take that away and you wipe me out.

LAURA: Why didn't we separate in time?

CAPTAIN: Because the child held us together, but the bond has become a chain. How has that happened? I've never thought about that sort of thing before, but now I begin to remember incidents that render you suspect, and perhaps condemn you. We'd been married for two years, and had no children – you know why not. I became ill, and was at death's door. Once, when the fever had abated for a while, I heard voices outside in the drawing-room. It was you and the lawyer, and you were talking about the property that I still owned in those days. He explained that you couldn't inherit anything because we had no children, and he asked if you were expecting one. I couldn't hear your answer. I recovered, and we had a child. Who is the father?

LAURA: You are!

CAPTAIN: No, I am not. There's a crime lying buried here that's beginning to stink – and what a hellish crime it is! You women pity black slaves and set them free, but you keep white ones. I've worked and slaved for you and your child, your mother, and your servants. I've sacrificed my career and promotion, I've been racked and tortured, I've endured sleepless nights, worrying about your future till my hair has turned grey, and all so that you could enjoy a carefree life, and when you grew old, live it again through your child. I've borne all this without complaining because I imagined that I was the father of that child. It was the lowest kind of theft – the most brutal slavery. I've served seventeen years' hard labour though I

THE FATHER

was innocent. What can you give me in return for that?

LAURA: Now you're really mad!

CAPTAIN [*sitting*]: That's what you hope. I've seen how you've struggled to hide your sin. I've sympathized with you, realizing what caused your anxiety; I've often lulled your guilty conscience to rest, thinking that I was chasing away some morbid fancy. I've heard you cry out in your sleep, and I've refused to listen. Now I remember the night before last – it was Bertha's birthday. It was between two and three in the morning and I was sitting up reading. You screamed 'Keep away, keep away!' as if someone were trying to strangle you. I knocked on the wall because – because I didn't want to hear any more. I'd had my suspicions for a long time, but I dared not hear them confirmed. That's how I've suffered for your sake; what will you do for me?

LAURA: What can I do? I swear before God and all that I hold sacred that you are Bertha's father.

CAPTAIN: What use is that, when you've already said that a mother can and should commit any crime for her child's sake? I implore you, for the sake of the past – I implore you, as a wounded man begs for the death-blow – tell me everything. Don't you see that I'm as helpless as a child? Can't you hear that I'm calling to you as if you were my mother? Won't you forget that I'm a grown man – a soldier whose word of command both men and beasts obey? I am a sick man, all I ask is pity; I surrender the symbols of my power, and pray for mercy on my life.

LAURA [*coming to him and laying her hand on his forehead*]: What's this? A man, and crying?

CAPTAIN: Yes, I'm crying, although I'm a man. Has not a man eyes? Has not a man hands, organs, dimensions, senses, affections, passions? Fed with the same food, hurt with the same weapons, warmed and cooled by the same winter and summer as a woman. If you prick us, do we not bleed; if you tickle us, do we not laugh; if you poison us, do we not die? Why

shouldn't a man complain, or a soldier cry? Because it's unmanly. What makes it unmanly?

LAURA: Cry then, child, and your mother will be with you
again. Do you remember that, when I first came into your
life, it was as a second mother. Your great strong body had no
fibre, you were like an overgrown child, as if you'd come into
the world too soon, or perhaps were unwanted.

CAPTAIN: Yes, that's how it was. My father and mother never
wanted me, so I was born without a will. When you and I became one I thought I was completing myself; that's how you
got the upper hand, so that I – although I was the commander
in barracks and on parade – when I was with you, I was the
one to take orders. So I grew used to looking up to you as a
superior, gifted being, listening to you as if I were your back-
ward child.

LAURA: That's true, and that's why I loved you as if you were
my own child. But you must surely have noticed how em-
barrassed I was whenever your feelings altered, and you presented yourself as my lover. The pleasure of your embraces
was always followed by remorse, as if my very blood were
ashamed. The mother had become the mistress. Ugh!

CAPTAIN: I saw that, but I never understood why. And when I
thought you despised me for my unmanliness, I wanted to win
you as a woman by being a man.

LAURA: Yes, and that's where you were wrong. The mother
was your friend, you see, while the woman was your enemy.
Love between the sexes is a battle. And don't imagine that I
gave myself to you; I didn't give, I took – just what I wanted.
But you had one advantage – I realized that, and I wanted you
to realize it too.

CAPTAIN: You always had the advantage. If I was awake, you
could hypnotize me so that I could neither see nor hear, but
only obey; you could give me a raw potato and convince me
that it was a peach; you could compel me to admire your
most childish remark as if it were a flash of genius; you could

have led me into crime, and even into petty meanness. For you had no understanding, and instead of carrying out my ideas, you did things in your own way. But when I eventually woke up and came to my senses, I realized how my honour was tarnished and I wanted to redeem it by some noble action – some achievement, some discovery, or an honourable suicide. I should have liked to go to the wars, but there were none. Then I immersed myself in science. And now, when I should be reaching out my hand to gather the fruits of success, you cut off my arm. I am dishonoured now and I can no longer live, for a man cannot live without honour.

LAURA: But a woman?

CAPTAIN: Yes, for she has her children, while he has not. But we, like the rest of mankind, lived our lives as heedless as babies, full of fancies, ideas, and illusions; till we finally woke. That was all very well, but we woke with our feet on the pillow, and whoever it was who woke us was a sleepwalker himself. When women grow old and cease to be women, they grow hair on their chins; I wonder what becomes of men when they grow old and cease to be men. Those who once crowed were no longer cocks but only capons, and the pullets answered the call, so that when it should have been sunrise, we found ourselves sitting among ruins in bright moonlight, just as in the good old days. It had only been a little morning nap, with bad dreams, and there was no awakening.

LAURA: You should have been a poet, you know.

CAPTAIN: Perhaps.

LAURA: Well, I'm sleepy, so if you've any more fancies, keep them till tomorrow.

CAPTAIN: One word first – about realities: do you hate me?

LAURA: Yes, sometimes – when you act like a man.

CAPTAIN: That's like racial prejudice. If it's true that we're descended from apes, it must at least have been from two different species. Certainly there's no resemblance between us.

LAURA: What do you mean by all this?

CAPTAIN: I realize that one of us must go under in this struggle.

LAURA: Which?

CAPTAIN: The weaker, of course.

LAURA: And the stronger will be in the right?

CAPTAIN: Naturally, since he has the power.

LAURA: Then I am in the right!

CAPTAIN: Have you the power already, then?

LAURA: Yes, legal power, too, and tomorrow I shall use it to put you under restraint.

CAPTAIN: Under restraint?

LAURA: Yes, then I shall bring up my child in my own way, without having to trouble about your whims.

CAPTAIN: And who will pay for her education when I'm gone?

LAURA: Your pension.

CAPTAIN [*advancing on her, threateningly*]: And how can you have me put under restraint?

LAURA [*taking out a letter*]: By means of this letter – of which an attested copy is in the hands of the Board of Guardians.

CAPTAIN: What letter?

LAURA [*backing towards the door on the left*]: This! Your admission to the doctor that you are insane. [*The* CAPTAIN *stares at her, dumbfounded.*] You've fulfilled your function, now, as the – unfortunately – essential father and breadwinner. There's no further need for you, and you must go. You must go because, though you've seen now that my intellect is as formidable as my will, you won't stay and acknowledge it!

[*The* CAPTAIN *goes to the table, takes up the lighted lamp and hurls it at* LAURA, *who backs quickly through the door.*]

CURTAIN

ACT THREE

[*The same setting as before, but with a different lamp. The private door is barricaded with a chair.*]

LAURA: Did he give you the keys?

NURSE: Give me them? No. God forgive me. I took them out of his clothes when Nöjd brought them out to brush.

LAURA: So it's Nöjd who's on duty today.

NURSE: Yes, it's Nöjd.

LAURA: Give me the keys.

NURSE: Very well, but it's as good as stealing. Just listen to him up there, pacing up and down, up and down.

LAURA: Is the door safely fastened?

NURSE: Oh yes, it's safe enough.

LAURA [*opening the desk and sitting at it*]: You must control yourself Margret. The only hope for all of us is to keep calm. [*There is a knock on the hall door.*] Who is it?

NÖJD: [*opening it*]: It's Nöjd.

LAURA: Let him come in.

NÖJD [*entering*]: There's a note from the Colonel.

LAURA: Give it to me. [*She reads.*] Ah . . . Nöjd, have you taken all the cartridges out of the guns and emptied the pouches?

NÖJD: I've done all you said, madam.

LAURA: Then wait outside while I answer the Colonel's letter.

[NÖJD *goes, and* LAURA *starts to write.*]

NURSE: Oh, hark, ma'am! Whatever is he doing up there?

LAURA: Be quiet, I'm writing.

[*A sound of sawing is heard.*]

NURSE: God have mercy on us! What'll be the end of this?

LAURA: There. Give this to Nöjd. And my mother's not to know anything about all this, do you understand?

[*The* NURSE *goes to the door.* LAURA *opens the desk drawers and takes out papers. The* PASTOR *enters and, drawing up a chair, sits beside* LAURA *at the desk.*]

PASTOR: Good evening, Laura, I've been out all day, I expect they told you; I've only just got home. Things have taken a serious turn here, then?

LAURA: Yes, my dear. I've never been through anything like this last twenty-four hours!

PASTOR: I see you're none the worse for it.

LAURA: No, thank heaven. But just think what might have happened.

PASTOR: Tell me, how did it all begin? I've heard so many different stories.

LAURA: It began with those absurd ideas of his about not being Bertha's father, and it ended with his throwing a lighted lamp in my face.

PASTOR: But that's appalling. He must be completely mad. What are we to do now?

LAURA: We must try to stop any more outbreaks – the doctor's sent to the hospital for a strait-jacket. In the meanwhile, I've sent a message to the Colonel, and now I'm trying to look into the household accounts, which he's mismanaged terribly.

PASTOR: It's a deplorable business, but I always expected something like this would happen; you can't mix fire and water without an explosion. What's all that in the drawer?

LAURA [*with a drawer she has opened*]: Just look at all the things he kept here!

PASTOR: Good heavens! Here's your doll – and here's your christening cap; and Bertha's rattle – and your letters and this locket. [*He wipes his eyes.*] He must have loved you very much, Laura, all the same. I've never kept things like this.

LAURA: I think he did love me once, but time – time changes so many things.

PASTOR: What's that big paper there? A receipt for a grave. Well, better a grave than an asylum. Laura, tell me: is your conscience quite clear in all this?

LAURA: Mine? How could I be to blame if a man goes out of his mind?

PASTOR: Ah well, I won't say anything. After all, blood's thicker than water.

LAURA: Just what do you mean by that?

PASTOR [*looking her straight in the face*]: Well . . .

LAURA: Yes?

PASTOR: Well, you can hardly deny that it would suit you very well if you could bring up your child in your own way.

LAURA: I don't understand.

PASTOR: I really admire you, Laura.

LAURA: Do you? Hm.

PASTOR: So I'm to become the guardian of that free-thinker. You know, I've always looked on him as a weed in our garden.

LAURA [*gives a short laugh, then immediately becomes serious*]: And you dare to say that to me, his wife?

PASTOR: How strong you are, Laura – incredibly strong! You're like a fox in a trap, you'd rather bite off your own leg than let yourself be caught. You're like a master-thief – you have no accomplice, not even your own conscience. Look at yourself in the glass! You dare not!

LAURA: I never look in a glass.

PASTOR: No, you dare not. Show me your hand: not one spot of blood to betray you – not a trace of subtle poison. A little innocent murder that the law cannot touch; an unconscious crime. 'Unconscious' – what a beautiful idea. Do you hear how he's working up there? Be careful! If that man ever gets loose, he'll saw you to pieces.

LAURA: You talk so much, you must have a guilty conscience. Accuse me, if you can!

PASTOR: I cannot.

LAURA: There you are, then! You cannot, so I am not guilty. And now, you take care of your ward, and I'll look after mine. Here's the Doctor. [*She rises.*] I'm glad to see you, Doctor; you, at any rate, will help me, won't you? Not that there's much to be done, I'm afraid. Do you hear how he's going on up there? Does *that* convince you?

DOCTOR: I'm convinced that he has become violent, but the question is whether the violence must be considered as an outbreak of rage or of madness.

PASTOR: Whatever caused the actual outbreak, you'll admit that he suffered from fixed ideas.

DOCTOR: I believe, Pastor, your own ideas are even more firmly fixed.

PASTOR: My firm convictions about higher things –

DOCTOR: Let us set aside convictions for the moment. Madam, it is for you to decide whether your husband is liable to imprisonment and a fine, or to go to an asylum. What have you to say about the Captain's behaviour?

LAURA: How can I answer that now?

DOCTOR: Then you have no firm convictions about what would be best for your family. What do *you* say, Pastor?

PASTOR: It's hard to say – there'll be a scandal either way.

LAURA: But if he's merely fined for assault, he might become violent again.

DOCTOR: And if he's sent to prison, he'll soon be out again. Therefore we feel it's in the best interests of all parties that he should be treated as insane at once. Where is the nurse?

LAURA: Why?

DOCTOR: I want her to put the strait-jacket on the patient after I've had a word with him, and when I give the order, but not before. I have the – garment outside. [*He goes out to the hall, and returns with a large parcel.*] Would you kindly ask the nurse to come in.

[LAURA *rings the bell.*]

PASTOR: Horrible, horrible!

[*The* NURSE *comes in.*]

DOCTOR [*unpacking the jacket*]: Now, pay attention, please. I want you to slip this waistcoat on the Captain from behind, as soon as I consider it necessary, so as to forestall any further outbreaks of violence. As you see, it has unusually long sleeves that can be tied behind the back to restrict his movements. And here we have two straps with buckles which you then make fast to the arms of the chair or sofa, whichever is more convenient. Will you do this?

NURSE: No, doctor, I couldn't, I couldn't!

LAURA: Why don't you do it yourself, Doctor?

DOCTOR: Because the patient mistrusts me. You, madam, should really be the one to do it, but I fear that he mistrusts even you. [LAURA frowns.] Perhaps the Pastor . . .

PASTOR: No, I must decline.

[NÖJD enters.]

LAURA: Did you deliver the note?

NÖJD: Yes, madam.

DOCTOR: Ah, Nöjd. You know the circumstances here. The Captain is out of his mind, and you must help us to look after our patient.

NÖJD: If there's anything I can do for the Captain, he knows I'll do it.

DOCTOR: You're to put this jacket on him –

NURSE: No! He shan't touch him – Nöjd might hurt him. I'd sooner do it myself, gently – very gently. But Nöjd can wait outside in case I need any help – yes, he can do that.

[There is hammering on the private door.]

DOCTOR: Here he is! Leave the jacket on that chair, with your shawl over it, and all wait outside, while the Pastor and I receive him. Quickly – that door won't hold much longer!

NURSE [going out left]: Lord help us!

[LAURA shuts the desk, then goes out left, NÖJD goes out at the back.]

[The private door is burst open, so that the lock is broken and the chair flung to the ground. The CAPTAIN comes in, with a pile of books under his arm; he puts them on the table.]

CAPTAIN: It's all to be found here – in every one of these books. So I wasn't mad after all. Here it is in the Odyssey – Book I, line

21 5; page 6 in the Uppsala translation. Telemachus is speaking to Athene. 'My mother indeed declares that he – meaning Odysseus – is my father; but I myself cannot be sure; since no man ever yet knew his own begetter.' And it was Penelope, the most virtuous of women, whom Telemachus was suspecting. That's a fine thing, eh? And then we have the prophet Ezekiel: 'The fool saith: Lo, here is my father, but who can tell whose loins have engendered him?' That's clear enough, isn't it? And what have we here? Merzlyakov's *History of Russian Literature*: Alexander Pushkin, Russia's greatest poet, died in agony caused much more by the rumours going round of his wife's infidelity than by the bullet wound in his chest from a duel. On his death-bed he swore that she was innocent. Ass! Ass! How could he swear to that. You see, by the way, that I can still read my books. Ah, Jonas, are you here? And the doctor, of course. Did I ever tell you what I said to an English lady who complained of the habit Irishmen have of throwing lighted lamps in their wives' faces? 'God, what women!' I said. 'Women?' she simpered. 'Yes, of course,' I answered. When things get to such a pitch that a man – a man who has loved and worshipped a woman – goes and takes a lighted lamp and flings it in her face . . . well, then you know.

PASTOR: What do you know?

CAPTAIN: Nothing. One never knows anything – one only believes – isn't that so, Jonas? One believes, and one is saved. Yes, that's how it is! But I know that a man's belief can destroy him – that's what I know!

DOCTOR: Captain –

CAPTAIN: Be quiet! I don't wish to speak to you – you're just a telephone, relaying all their chatter in there. Yes, in there– you know what I mean. Tell me, Jonas, do you believe that you're the father of your children? I remember you used to have a tutor in the house – a good-looking fellow that people used to gossip about.

PASTOR: Adolf – mind what you're saying.

CAPTAIN: Feel under your wig and see if you can't find two bumps there. Upon my soul I believe he's turned pale! Oh yes, it's only talk, of course, but heavens, how they do talk. But we're all laughing-stocks anyway, we married men, aren't we, doctor? How was your marriage bed? Wasn't there a young subaltern in your house, eh? Let me guess: his name was – [*he whispers in the* DOCTOR's *ear.*] There, you see, *he's* turned pale, too! But cheer up, she's dead and buried, and what's done can't be undone. I used to know him, by the way; he's now – look at me, Doctor . . . no, straight in the face – he's a major of Dragoons. Bless me if I don't believe you have horns too!

DOCTOR [*upset*]: Captain, please let us change the subject.

CAPTAIN: There you are! Directly I mentioned horns, he wants to change the subject.

PASTOR: Adolf, do you realize that you're not in your right senses?

CAPTAIN: Of course I realize it. But if I could work on your crowned heads for a little, I'd soon have you shut up, too. Yes, I'm mad; but what sent me mad? That doesn't interest you – nor anyone else. Do you want to change the subject now? [*He takes the photograph album from the table.*] Christ! That's my daughter! Is she mine? We can't be sure. Do you know what we'd have to do to be sure? Marry first, so as to be accepted by society, then separate directly after, and become lover and mistress, and then adopt the children. Then we could at least be sure they were our own adopted children, couldn't we? But how can all that help me now? How can anything help me, now that you've taken my hope of immortality from me? What use are science or philosophy to me, now that I have nothing to live for? What can I do with my life now that my honour's gone? I grafted my right arm, half my brain, and half my marrow, onto another stem, for I thought they would grow together and knit themselves into a more perfect tree; and then someone comes with a knife and cuts them down below the graft, so that now I'm only half a tree; but the other half goes on growing, with my arm and half my brain, while I wither away and die, because it was the best part of myself that I gave away. And now I *want* to die. Do what you like with me, I no longer exist.

[*The* DOCTOR *whispers to the* PASTOR, *and they go out left into the inner room. Directly they are gone,* BERTHA *comes in. The* CAPTAIN *sits hunched up at the table.*]

BERTHA [*going up to him*]: Are you ill, papa?

CAPTAIN [*looks up dully*]: I?

BERTHA: Do you know what you did? Do you know that you threw the lamp at Mama?

CAPTAIN: Did I?

BERTHA: Yes, you did! Suppose she'd been hurt.

CAPTAIN: Would it have mattered?

BERTHA: You aren't my father if you can say things like that!

CAPTAIN: What's that? I'm not your father? How do you know? Who told you so? Who *is* your father, then? Who is?

BERTHA: Well, not you, anyhow.

CAPTAIN: Always the same thing – not I! Who then, who? You seem to be well informed – who told you? That I should live to have my own child tell me to my face that I'm not her father. But don't you know that that's insulting your mother; don't you understand that, if it's true, it's shameful for her, too?

BERTHA: I won't have you saying anything bad about Mama.

CAPTAIN: That's right, cling together, all of you, against me. That's what you've done all along.

BERTHA: Papa!

CAPTAIN: Don't ever call me that again!

BERTHA: Papa – papa!

CAPTAIN [*drawing her to him*]: Bertha, dear, darling child – because you *are* my child – yes, nothing else would be possible – you *must* be. Anything else was just a morbid idea brought on the wind, like pestilence and fever. Look at me, so that I can see my soul in your eyes. But I see *her* soul, too! You have two

68

souls, and you love me with one, and hate me with the other. But you must love me only. You must have only one soul, or you will never have any peace, and nor shall I. You must have one thought only, the child of my thought; and only one will — mine!

BERTHA: But I don't want that, I want to be myself.

CAPTAIN: I won't let you. You see, I'm a cannibal, and I want to eat you. Your mother wanted to eat me, but she couldn't. I am Saturn, who ate his own children because it had been foretold that otherwise they would eat him. To eat or to be eaten — that is the question. Unless I eat you, you will eat me — you've already shown me your teeth. But don't be afraid, my darling child, I shan't do you any harm.

[*He goes to the gun-rack and takes down a revolver.*]

BERTHA [*trying to escape*]: Help! Mama, help! He's going to murder me!

NURSE [*coming in*]: Mr Adolf! What are you doing?

CAPTAIN [*examining the revolver*]: Did you take out the cartridges?

NURSE: Well, I did tidy them away, but you just sit quietly here, and I'll soon get them again. [*She takes the* CAPTAIN'S *arm and sits him in a chair, where he stays listlessly. Then she brings out the strait-jacket and stations herself behind him.* BERTHA *creeps out to the left.*] Now, Mr Adolf, I wonder if you remember when you were my dear little boy and I used to tuck you up at night and read you 'Gentle Jesus'? Do you remember how I used to get up in the night and get you a drink, and how I used to light the candle and tell you lovely stories when you had bad dreams and couldn't sleep? Do you remember?

CAPTAIN: Go on talking, Margret; it makes my head better. Go on talking.

NURSE: All right, but you must pay attention, then. Do you remember that time you took the big carving-knife to make boats with, and how I came in and had to play a trick on you to get the knife away? You were a silly little boy, and we had to play tricks on you, because you wouldn't believe we knew what was best for you. 'Give me that snake,' I said, 'or it'll bite!' And you let go of it there and then. [*She takes the revolver from the* CAPTAIN'S *hand.*] And the times you wouldn't get dressed when you ought to. I used to have to wheedle you and say you'd have a golden coat and be dressed like a prince. And then I'd take your little jacket and say 'In with your arms now – both of them!' And then I'd say, 'Now sit nice and quiet while I button it down the back'. [*She has put the jacket on him.*] And then I'd say: 'Get up, now, like a good boy, and walk across the room, so that I can see how it fits'. [*She leads him to the sofa.*] And then I'd say 'Now you must go to bed'.

CAPTAIN: What's that? Go to bed when he's just been dressed? Damnation! What have you done to me? [*He tries to free himself.*] Woman! You're as cunning as the devil! Who'd have thought you had the sense? [*He lies on the sofa.*] Caught, shorn and outwitted – they won't even let me die!

NURSE: Forgive me, Mr Adolf, forgive me. I had to stop you from killing your child.

CAPTAIN: Why not let me kill the child? Life's a hell, and death is the Kingdom of Heaven; children belong to Heaven.

NURSE: How do you know what happens after death!

CAPTAIN: That's the only thing we *do* know, it's *life* that we know nothing of. Oh, if only we could have known from the first!

NURSE: Mr Adolf, humble your stubborn heart, and pray to God for mercy – it's not too late even now. It wasn't too late for the thief on the Cross, when the Saviour said, 'Today shalt thou be with me in Paradise'.

CAPTAIN: Are you croaking for a corpse already, you old crow? [*The* NURSE *takes a hymn-book from her pocket. Calling*] Nöjd! Is Nöjd there? [NÖJD *enters.*] Throw that woman out. She wants to smother me with her hymn-book. Throw her out of the window – up the chimney – anywhere you like!

NÖJD [*looking at the* NURSE]: Heaven help you, Captain, really, but I can't do that, honestly I can't. I'd take on half a dozen men – but not a woman!

CAPTAIN: You can't get the better of a woman, eh?

NÖJD: Of course I can, but it's a different thing when it comes to laying hands on one.

CAPTAIN: What's so different about it? Haven't they been laying their hands on me?

NÖJD: Yes, but I can't do it, Captain. It's just as if you were to ask me to hit the pastor. It's something inside me – like religion. I can't do it.

[LAURA *enters; she signs to* NÖJD *to go.*]

CAPTAIN: Omphale! Omphale! Playing with the club while Hercules spins your wool!

LAURA [*coming to the sofa*]: Adolf – look at me. Do you believe that I'm your enemy?

CAPTAIN: Yes, I do! I believe that you're all my enemies. My mother, who didn't want to bring me into the world because my birth would bring her pain, she was my enemy: she starved my unborn life of its nourishment, till I was nearly deformed. My sister was my enemy, when she taught me to be her vassal. The first woman I took in my arms was my enemy, for she gave me ten years' illness in return for the love I gave her. My daughter became my enemy, when she had to choose between me and you. And you, my wife, you were my mortal enemy, for you never let me be till you had me lying dead.

LAURA: I don't know that the thoughts and motives that you're suggesting ever entered my head. It's possible that I was swayed by an obscure desire to be rid of you, as something that stood in my way; if you see some plan behind my actions – well, there may have been one, but I knew nothing about it. I've never considered them, they've simply run on the lines that you yourself have laid down, and, before God and my conscience, I feel myself innocent even if I am not. Your existence has been like a stone on my heart, weighing and weighing it down till the heart struggled to throw off the burden that oppressed it. That is how it was, and if I have harmed you unintentionally, I ask you to forgive me.

CAPTAIN: All that sounds very plausible, but how does it help me? And who is to blame? A spiritual marriage, perhaps? In the old days, a man married a wife, now he enters into partnership with a business-woman, or sets up house with a friend. Then he debauches the partner, and violates the friend. What becomes of love – healthy physical love? It dies in the process. And what is the issue of this love – in bonds payable to bearer, without joint liability? Who is the bearer when the crash comes? Who is the physical father of the spiritual child?

LAURA: As for your suspicions about the child, they're quite unfounded.

CAPTAIN: That is just what is so terrible. If there had been any foundation for them, that would at least be something to take hold of – to cling to; as it is, there are only shadows, that hide in the bushes and poke their heads out to grin. It's like hitting the air, or a sham fight with blank cartridges. A mortal truth would have roused my resistance, and roused my mind and body to action – but, as things are, my thoughts melt into thin air, and my brain grinds away at nothing, till it catches fire. Give me a pillow under my head. And put something over me, I'm cold – terribly cold.

[LAURA takes her shawl and spreads it over him; the NURSE goes to fetch a pillow.]

LAURA: Give me your hand, my dear.

CAPTAIN: My hand? When you've tied it behind my back? Omphale! Omphale! But I can feel your soft shawl against my mouth, it's as warm and soft as your arm, and it smells of vanilla like your hair when you were young. . . . When you were young, Laura, and we used to walk in the birchwoods among the primroses and the thrushes – lovely – lovely! Think how beautiful life was, and what it is now. You never wanted it to come to this, and nor did I; yet this has happened. Who orders our lives?

LAURA: Only God. . . .

CAPTAIN: The god of Strife, then – or is it a goddess these days? Take away this cat that's lying on me – take it away! [*The* NURSE *comes in with the pillow, and takes away the shawl.*] Give me my tunic – put that over me. [*The* NURSE *takes the tunic from the peg and puts it over him.*] Ah, my rough lion-skin that you tried to take away from me. Omphale! Omphale! You cunning woman – who wanted peace and preached disarmament. Wake up, Hercules, or they'll take your club from you. You'd trick us out of our armour, too, making believe it was tinsel. No, it was iron, iron, before it became tinsel. In the olden days it was the smith who forged the coat of mail, now it's the sempstress. Omphale! Omphale! Rude strength is brought down by scheming weakness. Damn you, you she-devil, curse your whole sex! [*He raises himself to spit, but falls back on the sofa.*] What sort of pillow have you given me, Margret? It's so hard and cold – so cold. Come and sit beside me – here, on the chair. That's it. Let me put my head on your lap. There! Ah, that's warmer. Lean over me, so that I can feel your breast. Oh, it's good to sleep on a woman's breast – a mother's or a mistress's, but a mother's is best.

LAURA: Do you want to see your child, Adolf? Do you?

CAPTAIN: My child? A man doesn't have children, it's only women who get children. That's why the future is theirs, and we die childless.

> 'Gentle Jesus, meek and mild,
> Look upon a little child –'

NURSE: Listen, he's praying to God!

CAPTAIN: No, to *you* – to put me to sleep. I'm tired – so tired. Good night, Margret! And blessed be thou among women.

    [*He raises himself, but falls back with a cry on the* NURSE'S *knees.* LAURA *goes to the left and calls to the* DOCTOR, *who enters with the* PASTOR.]

LAURA: Help, Doctor, if it's not too late. Look, he's stopped breathing.

DOCTOR [*feeling the patient's pulse*]: It's a stroke.

PASTOR: Is he dead?

DOCTOR: No, he may still recover consciousness — but what sort of consciousness we don't know.

PASTOR: First death, and after that the Judgement. . . .

DOCTOR: No judgement. No indictment, even! You believe there's a god who rules man's destiny, you must refer this affair to Him.

NURSE: Pastor — in his last moments he prayed to God.

PASTOR [*to* LAURA]: Is that true?

LAURA: Quite true.

DOCTOR: In that case — and I can no more judge of that, than I can of the cause of his illness — then there's nothing more that my skill can do. It's up to you to try yours now, Pastor.

LAURA: Is that all you have to say at this death-bed, Doctor?

DOCTOR: Yes, that's all I know. If anyone knows more, let him speak!

BERTHA [*coming in, left, and running to her mother*]: Mama! Mama!

LAURA: My child — my own child!

PASTOR: Amen.

CURTAIN

MISS JULIA

A NATURALISTIC PLAY

(1888)

In *Miss Julia*, writing the year after *The Father*, when his separation from Siri von Essen was less raw, Strindberg could deal more objectively with the struggle between the sexes. Here he has added to it another battle that was continually raging within himself – that of the aristocratic blood inherited from his father, warring against 'the blood of the slave' that came from his adored mother. He had had ample chance of observing the ways of servants and their relations with their masters, for even when his family was at its poorest, Strindberg's father insisted on keeping two servants in the overcrowded household – who, he tells us, were not allowed to clean their master's boots unless they wore gloves!

He gained further experience of servants in his last year at school, when poverty drove him to spend his summer holidays as a tutor to a Baron's sons on a country estate. Here the family patronized him, and the servants were insolent to him, making it very clear that they thought him no better than themselves. He spent Midsummer Night of 1862 there, and the impudent 'Jean', with his Frenchified name, may well have been suggested by one of the staff. (Incidentally, Strindberg's own first name was Johann.) In the grounds too, he may have seen just such an exotic little earth-closet as he has put into this play, and that must seem so strange to an English audience, and even English actors, that many of them probably miss the point of it altogether.

An incident two years later, in 1864, shows how violently the two inheritances fought within him. He was living comfortably (for once) as tutor in a rich and cultured Jewish family, when one night during dinner some political demonstrators passed the window. When someone explained to a foreign visitor that they were 'only the mob', Strindberg jumped up from the table and rushed out of the house, feeling that he was a deserter from his own (or at least his mother's) people.

Strindberg wrote a long preface to this play, setting out his ideas on naturalism in drama. Much of it seems rather obvious to us in these days when out theatre is only just beginning to emerge from a period of excessive naturalism, but in 1888 it was exciting and revolutionary. We must remember that Strindberg's audience was accustomed to seeing such things as the kitchen dresser and its utensils merely painted on the backcloth. It would have been fresh and exciting to them not only to hear the players speaking everyday language, but also to see an actress moving naturally about the kitchen, tidying up dishes; though nowadays, in production, Kristin's long bit of 'business' is usually whittled down to as little as will suggest the necessary lapse of time. To us, too, it seems odd that Strindberg should specially mention that she should even turn her back 'when necessary', and we must remember that even in the West End of London in the 1920s Sir John Martin-Harvey could reproach an actress of the younger school in his company, saying: 'You must *never* turn your back on the audience'.

The play's action is continuous; Strindberg was developing a theory, later discarded, that the division of the play into acts, with the necessary fall of the curtain, shattered the illusion. His complaint that intervals were only an excuse for the bars to make money sounds topical even today. However, he has not been entirely successful in dealing with the unity of time, and ingenious as Kristin's 'business' and the incursion of the peasants may be as technical tricks, in practice they interrupt the action quite as much as would the fall of a curtain.

· · ·

This translation of Miss Julia *was originally made for the British Broadcasting Corporation, with whose consent it has been used here.*

MISS JULIA

CHARACTERS

MISS JULIA, *aged 25*
'JEAN', *a footman, aged 30*
KRISTIN, *a cook*

The action takes place in the Count's kitchen, on
Midsummer Eve

[*A large kitchen, with the ceiling and side-walls masked by draperies.
The back-wall runs diagonally across the stage from down left to up
right. On this wall to the left are two shelves, decorated with scalloped
paper, and filled with copper, iron, and tin utensils. Rather to the right,
most of a big arched outer doorway is visible; it has two glass doors,
through which are seen a fountain with a Cupid, lilacs in flower, and tall
poplar trees. To the left is the corner of a big tiled stove, with part of its
hood showing. From the right, the end of a pinewood kitchen-table
sticks out, with a chair or two. The stove is decorated with bunches of
birch-twigs, and the floor is strewn with juniper. On the table-end is a
big Japanese ginger-jar of lilac. There is also an ice-box, a dresser, and
a sink.*

*Over the door, a big old-fashioned bell hangs on a spring, and the
mouthpiece of a speaking-tube is visible to the left of the door.*

KRISTIN *is standing at the stove, cooking in a frying-pan. She is
wearing an apron over her light cotton dress.* JEAN *comes in — he is in
livery, and carries a pair of big riding-boots with spurs, which he
puts down where they can be seen.*]

JEAN: Miss Julia's mad again tonight — completely mad.
KRISTIN: Oh, so you're back, are you?
JEAN: I took the Count to the station, and on the way back by

the barn I looked in and joined the dancing. Well, there was Miss Julia – and leading the dance, with the gamekeeper of all people! The minute she saw me, she rushed right up and asked me to dance the ladies' waltz with her. And how she waltzed, too; I've never known anything like it! She's off her head.

KRISTIN: That's nothing new! But she's been carrying on worse than ever this last fortnight – since her engagement was broken off. . . .

JEAN: And what a story that was! He seemed a decent sort of fellow, too – not much money, though. But you know what they are once they get an idea in their heads. [*He sits down at the end of the table.*] Queer, isn't it, for a young lady – ahem – to want to stay here with the servants – rather than go with her father to see her cousins.

KRISTIN: She's probably ashamed to face them after the to-do with her young man.

JEAN: I shouldn't wonder. He knew how to stand up to her, that fellow. D'you know what happened, Kristin? I saw the whole thing – though I pretended not to notice.

KRISTIN: What? You *saw* it?

JEAN: I certainly did. They were down in the stable-yard, and she was 'training' him – as she called it. And what do you think she was doing? She was making him jump over her riding-whip – just like teaching a dog tricks. He jumped it twice, and each time she caught him a stinger with the whip. And then the third time, he wrenched it out of her hand, broke it in pieces, and then cleared out.

KRISTIN: Did he, though? Well, I never!

JEAN: Yes; so that was the end of that! Got anything nice to eat for me, Kristin?

KRISTIN [*taking something from the frying-pan and putting it in front of* JEAN]: Just a scrap of kidney – I cut it out of the joint for you.

JEAN [*smelling it*]: Lovely! – That's just *ce que j'adore*! [*Feels the*

79

plate.] Here, you might have warmed the plate, though!

KRISTIN: You're faddier than the Count, even, once you start. [*She strokes his hair tenderly.*]

JEAN [*irritably*]: Hey, you'd better leave me alone – you know how easily I get worked up.

KRISTIN: All right – only I do love you, you know.

[JEAN *eats.* KRISTIN *gets out a bottle of beer.*]

JEAN: What, beer on Midsummer Eve? No thanks! I can do better than that myself. [*He opens a drawer and takes out a bottle of red wine with a gold seal.*] There, you see – Gold Seal! Give me a glass – a wine-glass of course – since I'm having it neat.

KRISTIN [*putting a small saucepan on the stove*]: Heaven help the woman that gets you for a husband; I never knew such a fusspot.

JEAN: Nonsense, you'd be glad enough to get me; it's even done you a bit of good to be known as the sweetheart of a smart chap like me. [*Tastes the wine.*] This is excellent – excellent. Might be just a shade warmer. [*He warms the glass between his hands.*] We bought this in Dijon – four francs a litre, from the wood – and then the duty on top of that. What's that you're cooking? It stinks the place out.

KRISTIN: Oh, it's some devil's brew that Miss Julia wants, it's for Diana.

JEAN: You ought to watch your language, Kristin. Anyway, why should you be cooking for a blasted dog – on a holiday, too! Is it ill?

KRISTIN: She's ill all right. She's been running round with the dog at the lodge, and now she's got herself into trouble. My lady won't stand for that, you know.

JEAN: My lady's finicky enough over some things, a pity she isn't over others. Just like the Countess when she was alive! She was most at home in the kitchen or the cowsheds – but she'd never drive with only one horse. She'd have dirty cuffs, but the buttons had to have the coronet on them. And now here's Miss Julia; she doesn't keep her clothes clean either –

or herself, for that matter. Not refined, if you ask me. Why, out in the barn just now, the gamekeeper was dancing with Anna, and she comes up and grabs him and asks him to dance with *her*. *We*'d never do a thing like that. But that's what happens when the gentry go slumming – they get slummy. She's a fine-looking girl, though; fine – a good pair of shoulders – and so on.

KRISTIN: Oh, she isn't all that fine; Clara dresses her, and you ought to hear what *she* says.

JEAN: Clara? Pooh, you women are always jealous. *I*'ve been out riding with her – and I've seen her dance.

KRISTIN: Jean, will you dance with me, when I've finished this?

JEAN: Of course.

KRISTIN: Promise?

JEAN: Why? If I say I'll do a thing, I do it. [*Rising.*] Anyhow – thanks for the supper, it was very tasty.

[*He corks the bottle again.*]

MISS JULIA [*she appears in the door, talking to someone outside*]: I'll be back in a minute – don't wait for me.

[JEAN *slips the bottle in the table drawer, and rises respectfully.*]

MISS JULIA [*coming in – she goes over to* KRISTIN *who is at the mirror*]: Well, is it ready yet?

[KRISTIN *signs to her that* JEAN *is there.*]

JEAN [*gallantly*]: Do you ladies want to talk secrets?

MISS JULIA [*flipping him in the face with her handkerchief*]: It's no business of yours.

JEAN: What a lovely scent of violets!

MISS JULIA [*coquetting*]: Impertinence! So you know about scent too? You certainly know how to dance, don't you. Now, go away; you're not to peep –

JEAN [*impudent without being rude*]: I suppose it's the sort of witch's brew that ladies cook up on Midsummer Night – something to tell fortunes with, and show you the face of your future husband.

MISS JULIA: [*sharply*]: You'd need good eyes to see *that*. [*To* KRISTIN]: Put it in a bottle, and cork it properly. Now then, Jean, come out again and dance the schottische with me.

JEAN [*doubtfully*]: Well – no offence, but I promised this one to Kristin.

MISS JULIA: Oh, she can dance with you any time – can't you, Kristin? You don't mind lending him to me, do you?

KRISTIN: I know my place, my lady. If you're so kind, it isn't for Jean to say no. [*Turns*] Get along with you, Jean, you ought to be honoured.

JEAN: Well, I don't want to speak out of turn – but, to put it plainly, would it be quite the thing for my lady to dance with the same partner twice running? You know how people round here talk –

MISS JULIA [*flaring up*]: Talk? Why should they talk? What do you mean?

JEAN [*respectfully*]: Well, Miss Julia, if you won't see what I mean . . . To put it bluntly, it wouldn't do to go out of your way to favour one of your servants, when all the rest are expecting you to honour them.

MISS JULIA: Favour? I've never heard of such a thing. I'm the mistress here, and if I condescend to go to the servants' ball when I feel like dancing, I shall dance with someone who can lead, and not make me look ridiculous.

JEAN: As you say, Miss Julia – I'm at your service.

MISS JULIA [*softly*]: You mustn't take it as an order; it's a holiday tonight – everyone ought to enjoy themselves – not think about rank. Give me your arm. Don't worry, Kristin – I'm not going to steal your young man.

[JEAN *gives her his arm and leads her out.*]

[*The following stage-business should be played as if the actress were really alone in the room. When it is natural for her to turn her back on the audience she must do so; she must not look out into the auditorium, nor should she hurry as if she were afraid the public might grow impatient.*]

KRISTIN *is alone. A violin is heard faintly in the distance playing a schottische, and* KRISTIN *hums the tune while she clears up after* JEAN, *washing the plate at the sink, wiping it, and putting it away in a cupboard. Then she takes off her apron, and, bringing out a little mirror from one of the drawers in the table, she props it against the jar of lilac on the table. Then, lighting a tallow candle, she heats a hairpin and curls her fringe with it.*

Then she goes to the door and stands listening. As she comes back to the table, she notices the handkerchief which MISS JULIA *has left. She picks it up and smells it, then she spreads it out reflectively, smoothes it, and folds it in four, and so on.*]

JEAN [*coming in alone*] : She really must be mad, to go dancing like that – with everyone getting behind the doors and grinning at her. Don't you think so, Kristin?

KRISTIN: Well, you know how it is – she's always a bit queer at these times. What about our dance now?

JEAN: You didn't mind me going off like that? – Leaving you in the lurch.

KRISTIN: What was there to mind? Besides, I know my place.

JEAN [*slipping an arm around her waist*] : You're a sensible girl, Kristin – you'll make a good wife.

MISS JULIA [*enters. She is hurt and angry, but she speaks with a forced gaiety*] : Well, you're a fine escort! Running off and leaving your partner like that!

JEAN: On the contrary, Miss Julia, you see I've come running back to the partner I'd deserted.

MISS JULIA [*changing her tactics*] : You know, there's no one here can dance like you. But why are you wearing your livery? It's a holiday – go and change it at once.

JEAN: Then I must ask you to leave me a minute, my best coat's on that hook there.

[*He points to it, and goes over to the right.*]

MISS JULIA: Are you so bashful you can't even change your

coat in front of me? All right, go to your room and do it. Or stay here, and I'll turn my back!

JEAN: If you'll excuse me, Miss Julia –

[*He goes off right, but we see his arm as he changes the coat.*]

MISS JULIA: Well, Kristin, you seem very friendly with Jean – is he your sweetheart?

KRISTIN: Sweetheart! Yes, I suppose you could call it that.

MISS JULIA: You 'suppose'?

KRISTIN: Well, you know how it is, Miss Julia; after all, *you* were –

MISS JULIA: I was properly engaged.

KRISTIN: Still, it didn't come to anything, did it?

[*JEAN returns, in a black morning coat and a bowler hat.*]

MISS JULIA: *Très gentil, Monsieur Jean, très gentil!*

JEAN: *Vous voulez plaisanter, madam!*

MISS JULIA: *Et vous voulez parler français?* Where did you pick that up?

JEAN: In Switzerland; I was a waiter in one of the best hotels in Lucerne.

MISS JULIA: You look quite a gentleman in that coat – *charmant!*

[*She sits at the table.*]

JEAN: You flatter me.

MISS JULIA [*hurt*]: Flatter – you?

JEAN: My natural modesty forbids me to believe such a compliment to a man in my station. So I can only suppose that you are exaggerating – or, in other words, flattering.

MISS JULIA: Where did you learn to talk like that? Are you a great theatre-goer?

JEAN: Oh, yes. I've been about a bit, you know.

MISS JULIA: But you were born here, weren't you?

JEAN: My father was a farm-hand on the County Attorney's estate here. I used to see you when you were little; you never noticed me, though.

MISS JULIA: Really?

JEAN: Yes, I remember one time in particular – but I can't tell you about *that*.

MISS JULIA: Oh, do. Come on – I want you to.

JEAN: No, I couldn't possibly. Some other time, perhaps.

MISS JULIA: What's the use of 'some other time'? Was it as bad as all that?

JEAN: Not bad – I'd sooner not, that's all. Oh, look at her!

[*He points to* KRISTIN, *who has dropped off to sleep in a chair by the stove.*]

MISS JULIA: A nice sort of wife she'll make; she probably snores, too.

JEAN: No, but she talks in her sleep.

MISS JULIA [*cynically*]: How do *you* know?

JEAN [*boldly*]: I've heard her.

MISS JULIA [*their eyes meet for a moment*]: Why don't you sit down?

JEAN: I wouldn't take the liberty – not in your presence.

MISS JULIA: Supposing I order you?

JEAN: Then I'd obey.

MISS JULIA: Sit down, then. Wait a minute, though – can't you give me something to drink first?

JEAN: I don't know what there is in the ice-box – probably only beer.

MISS JULIA: 'Only' beer? I have very simple tastes – I'd rather have beer than wine.

[*He takes a bottle of beer from the ice-box, and opens it. He looks in the cupboard for a glass, and for a plate to serve it on.*]

JEAN: Allow me.

MISS JULIA: Thank you. Won't you have one too?

JEAN: I don't care much for beer, but if you tell me to –

MISS JULIA: Tell you! Surely a gentleman should keep a lady company.

JEAN: Yes, you're quite right.

[*He fetches a glass, and opens another bottle.*]

MISS JULIA: Now drink my health. [JEAN *hesitates.*] Don't tell me a big fellow like you is shy?

JEAN [*he kneels with mock-gallantry, and raises his glass*]: To my lady's health!

MISS JULIA: Bravo! Now you must kiss my shoe, to complete the picture. [JEAN *hesitates a moment, then boldly grasps her foot, which he kisses lightly.*] Well done! You should have been on the stage.

JEAN [*getting up*]: We can't go on like this, Miss Julia – suppose someone came in and saw us.

MISS JULIA: What would that matter?

JEAN: People talk, that's all! If you knew how their tongues were wagging up there just now –

MISS JULIA: What were they saying? Tell me. And sit down again.

JEAN [*sitting*]: Well, I don't want to speak out of turn, but they used expressions – that hinted that – well, you're not a child, you know what I mean. And when a lady drinks with a man – and a servant, at that – alone at night – then . . .

MISS JULIA: Then what? Besides, we aren't alone, Kristin's here.

JEAN: Yes, asleep.

MISS JULIA: I'll wake her, then. [*Getting up*]: Kristin, are you asleep?

KRISTIN [*mumbles*] – mm – mm –

MISS JULIA: Kristin! She can certainly sleep!

KRISTIN [*in her sleep*]: The Count's boots are done – mus' put on the coffee – just coming – my – pff . . .

MISS JULIA [*pulling her nose*]: Wake *up*.

JEAN [*sternly*]: Don't disturb her.

MISS JULIA [*sharply*]: What do you mean?

JEAN: She's been standing over the stove all day, of course she's tired by now. You ought to consider her a bit.

MISS JULIA [*changing her tone*]: That's a very kind thought – of course you're right – thank you. [*During the next few speeches,* KRISTIN *wakes, and still half dazed, goes off to the right to bed.*] Let's go out and you can pick me some lilac.

JEAN: Go out together, Miss Julia?

MISS JULIA: Of course.

JEAN: That wouldn't do at all. Never.

MISS JULIA: I don't see why not. You surely didn't imagine –

JEAN: Me? No – but the others'd think –

MISS JULIA: What? That I'm in love with a footman?

JEAN: Well, don't think I'm conceited, but it has been known to happen. And nothing's sacred to those people.

MISS JULIA: I do believe you're an aristocrat!

JEAN: Yes, I am.

MISS JULIA: Well, if I choose to step down –

JEAN: Don't, Miss Julia; no one'll ever believe you stepped down, they'll say you fell.

MISS JULIA: I've a better opinion of people than you have. Come and see if I'm not right. Come on.

[*She challenges him with her eyes.*]

JEAN: You're a queer one, you know.

MISS JULIA: Perhaps – so are you, if it comes to that. Anyhow, everything's queer – life, humanity, everything. It's just scum floating round and round on the top of the water – till it finally sinks. There's a dream I have every now and again, and this reminds me of it. I seem to have climbed to the top of a high pillar, and I sit there not knowing how to get down. If I look down it makes me dizzy, but I know I've got to get down somehow. I don't have the courage to jump. I can't hold on, though, and I wish I could fall, but I don't fall. Yet I know I won't get any peace or rest till I'm on the ground – right down on the ground. And I know that if I *were* down, I should want to go deeper and deeper into the earth. Do you ever feel like that?

JEAN: No – in *my* dream, I'm in a dark wood, lying under a tall tree. I want to get up – right to the top, where I can see out over the country in the sunlight. I want to rob the nest that holds the golden egg. And I climb and climb, but the trunk's so smooth and thick, and the lowest branch is so far out of reach. I know, though, that if I could only get hold of it, I could climb to the top as easy as up a ladder. I haven't got hold of it yet, but I will one day – even if it's only in a dream.

MISS JULIA: Here I am chattering to you about dreams! Come on – only as far as the park.

[*She gives him her arm, and they start to go.*]

JEAN: We ought to sleep on nine midsummer flowers tonight, Miss Julia, and then our dreams'd come true.

[*They turn as they reach the door.* JEAN *puts his hand up to one eye.*]

MISS JULIA: Something in your eye? Let me look.

JEAN: It's nothing – just a bit of dust. It'll be all right in a minute.

MISS JULIA: I must have flicked it with my sleeve. Sit down and I'll get it out for you. [*She takes his arm, and makes him sit down, then, gripping his head she bends it back, and tries to get out the bit of dust with a corner of her handkerchief.*] Now keep still. Still, I said! [*She slaps him on the hand.*] *Now* will you do as I tell you? I believe you're trembling – a big strong fellow like you. [*She feels his muscle.*] And with such arms!

JEAN [*with a note of warning*]: Miss Julia!

MISS JULIA: Yes, Monsieur Jean?

JEAN: *Attention, je ne suis qu'un homme!*

MISS JULIA: *Will* you sit still. There, that's out. Kiss my hand and say thank you!

JEAN [*rising*]: Miss Julia, listen, Kristin's gone to bed now. Won't you listen to what I say?

MISS JULIA: Kiss my hand first.

JEAN: Listen to me.

MISS JULIA: Kiss my hand first.

JEAN: All right – but you'll only have yourself to blame.

MISS JULIA: What for?

JEAN: 'What for'? You're not a child, you're twenty-five; don't you know it's dangerous to play with fire?

MISS JULIA: Not for me – I'm insured!

JEAN [*boldly*]: Oh no you're not – and even if you were, there's lots of inflammable stuff about.

MISS JULIA: Meaning yourself?

JEAN: Yes. Not because it's me, but because I'm young –

MISS JULIA: – and handsome! Aren't you conceited! I suppose you're a Don Juan! Or a Joseph! Yes, that's it, I believe you're a Joseph.

JEAN: Do you?

MISS JULIA: I'm beginning to be afraid you are. [JEAN *goes boldly up to her, and putting his arm round her waist, tries to give her a kiss. Slapping his face*] Hands off, now!

JEAN: Did you mean that, or are you playing with me?

MISS JULIA: I meant it.

JEAN: Then you meant what happened just before, too. You're taking the game much too seriously, and that's dangerous. Well, I'm tired of playing – if you'll excuse me, I'll get on with my work. It's long past midnight, and I have the Count's boots to do.

MISS JULIA: Put those boots down.

JEAN: No, that's my job, and I'm going to do it; it's no part of my duty to be a playmate for you, and I never will be, I've too much self-respect for that.

MISS JULIA: You're proud, aren't you.

JEAN: In some ways. Not in others.

MISS JULIA: Have you ever been in love?

JEAN: Well, we don't put it like that. I've been keen on lots of girls. Once, I was quite ill because I couldn't have the one I wanted – like the princes in the Arabian Nights who were so lovesick they couldn't eat or drink.

MISS JULIA: Who was she? [JEAN *is silent.*] Who was she?

JEAN: You'll never make me tell you.

MISS JULIA: Not if I ask you as an equal – as a friend? Who was she?

JEAN: You.

MISS JULIA [*sitting down again*]: That's a fine thing!

JEAN: Yes, if you like – quite ridiculous. That was the story I wouldn't tell you a few minutes ago – but now I'm going to. You don't know how the world looks from down below, do you? No – of course you don't, any more than hawks or eagles do; and we don't see their backs, because they're nearly always soaring up over our heads. I used to live in a hovel with seven brothers and sisters and a pig; out on the waste land where there wasn't even a tree. But the window used to look out on the wall of your father's park, and I could see the apple trees over it. I used to think it was the Garden of Eden, with all the fierce angels guarding it with fiery swords. All the same, the other boys and I found our way to the Tree of Life. I suppose you despise me.

MISS JULIA: Oh, all boys steal apples.

JEAN: You say that now, but you *do* despise me. Not that I care. Anyhow, one day my mother took me into the garden – it was to weed the onion-beds. Near the kitchen-garden there was a Turkish pavilion under the jasmine bushes, with honeysuckle growing over it. I didn't know what it could be used for, but it was the finest building I'd ever seen. People went in and out, and once, one of them came out and left the door open. I peeped in. The walls were covered with pictures of kings and emperors, and there were red curtains, with tassels, at the windows. You realize now the place I mean? Well, I – [*He breaks off a sprig of lilac, and holds it under her nose.*] I'd never been inside the castle – never been anywhere except the church, and this was much finer. Try as I might, I couldn't get it out of my mind, – that certain place, and bit by bit I got an overwhelming desire to know, just once, the full luxury of – *Enfin*, I sneaked in, and saw, and marvelled! Then I heard someone coming. There was only one way out for the gentry, of course, but for me there was another – and there was nothing for it but to use *that*. [MISS JULIA, *who has taken the lilac sprig, lets it fall on the table.*] Once I'd crawled out, I started to run; I crashed through the raspberry canes, ran over a strawberry patch and out into the rose garden. There I caught sight of a pink dress, and a pair of white stockings – it was you! I crawled under a pile of weeds – right into it; you can imagine what it was like, sharp thistles and wet stinking soil. And I watched you walking among the rose trees. And I thought, 'If it's true that a thief could go to paradise and live with the angels, it's odd that, here on God's earth, a poor farm lad like me can't go into the castle grounds and play with the Count's daughter'.

MISS JULIA [*sentimentally*]: Do you think all poor children would have felt like that?

JEAN [*hesitating at first, then with certainty*]: *All* poor . . .? Yes, of course, of course.

MISS JULIA: It must be terrible to be poor.

JEAN [*much moved, and with great emphasis*]: Oh, Miss Julia – a dog can lie on her ladyship's sofa, a horse can have his nose stroked by a young lady's hand, but a servant . . . (*in a different tone*) – Oh, now and then you find one with enough push to work his way up in the world, but how often does that happen? Anyhow, do you know what I did then? I jumped into the mill-stream with all my clothes on, and they fished me out and gave me a thrashing. But the next Sunday, when my father and everyone else at home were going over to my grandmother's, I managed it so that I stayed behind. I scrubbed myself with soap and hot water, and put my best clothes on, and went to church so as to catch a glimpse of you. I saw you, and made up my mind to go home and die. Only I wanted to die some beautiful, pleasant way, with no pain. Then I remembered that it was dangerous to sleep under an elder-tree. We had a big one in full bloom, so I pulled all the flowers off and put them in the oat-bin and made a bed for myself. Have you ever noticed how smooth oats are – It's like touching human skin. Well, I pulled the lid down and shut my eyes and went to sleep – only I didn't die, as you can see, but I woke up feeling very ill. I don't know what it was I wanted, really; there wasn't the slightest hope of winning you, of course; but you stood for the utter hopelessness of ever rising out of the class where I was born.

MISS JULIA: You know, you tell it very well – did you ever go to school?

JEAN: For a while. But I've read a lot of novels, and I go to the theatre. Besides, I've listened to better-class people talking – that's where I've learnt the most.

MISS JULIA: Do you stand there listening to what we say?

JEAN: Of course! And I've heard a lot, too – when I've been on the box of the carriage, or rowing the boat. I once heard you, Miss, and one of your young lady friends –

MISS JULIA: Oh! What did you hear?

JEAN: Well, I wouldn't like to tell you. But it was a bit of an eye-opener; I couldn't think where you'd learnt such words. Perhaps, after all, there isn't as much difference as they think between your class and mine.

MISS JULIA: You ought to be ashamed of yourself. *We* do at least behave ourselves when we're engaged.

JEAN [*looking her in the eye*]: Are you quite sure? There's no point in my lady playing the innocent with me.

MISS JULIA: The man I was in love with was a beast.

JEAN: That's what you all say – afterwards.

MISS JULIA: All?

JEAN: So it seems. Anyhow, I've heard plenty of girls say it –at times like that.

MISS JULIA: What times?

JEAN: The kind we're talking about. Let's see – the last time –

MISS JULIA [*getting up*]: Stop! I won't hear any more.

JEAN: She wouldn't, either. How odd! Well, if you'll excuse me, I'll go to bed.

MISS JULIA [*softly*]: What, go to bed on Midsummer Night?

JEAN: Yes, dancing with that crowd out there really doesn't amuse me.

MISS JULIA: Then get the key of the boathouse and row me out on the lake. I want to see the sunrise.

JEAN: Would that be wise?

MISS JULIA: You seem very careful about your reputation.

JEAN: What if I am? I don't want to be made to look a fool – or be thrown out without a reference; you see, I mean to get on in the world. Besides, I feel I ought to think of Kristin.

MISS JULIA: Oh, so it's Kristin now!

JEAN: Yes, but I'm thinking of you too. If you take my advice, you'll go to bed.

MISS JULIA: Do you think I'm going to be ordered about by you?

JEAN: Just this once – it's for your own good. Please! It's getting very late, and you can lose your head with sleepiness just as much as with wine. Do go to bed. Besides – listen – that sounds as if the others are coming to look for me. If they find us together, you're done for.

[*The song of the villagers is heard approaching.*]

VOICES: A lady walked in the wood so true –
Sing fol dol derry dol day-oh –
      And in the wood she . . . lost her shoe!
Singing fol dol derry dol day.

      'Oh, wed me soon', the maid did say –
Sing fol dol derry dol day-oh –
      ' 'Tis half a year since we did stray –'
Singing fol dol derry dol day.

      'This snowy wreath', her love replied –
Sing fol dol derry dol day-oh –
      'Last week bestowed I on my bride.'
Singing fol dol derry dol day.

MISS JULIA: I know my people. I love them, and they love me. Let them come in, and you'll see.

JEAN: No, Miss Julia, they don't love you. They take the food you give them, but as soon as your back's turned, they spit! That's the truth. Listen – can't you hear what they're singing? No, don't listen to them.

MISS JULIA [*listening*]: What is it?

JEAN: It's a dirty song – about you and me.

MISS JULIA: How disgusting! The filthy cowards.

JEAN: The rabble are always cowards. The only way to fight them is to run away.

MISS JULIA: But where? We can't get out now – and we can't go to Kristin's room.

JEAN: Well then, into mine – there's nothing else for it. You can trust me; I'm your friend, and I shall respect you – honestly I will.

MISS JULIA: But . . . suppose they looked for you there?

JEAN: I'll bolt the door, and if they try to break it down, I'll shoot. [*on his knees*] Do come, I beg you!

MISS JULIA [*significantly*]: And you promise me –

JEAN: I swear it.

[MISS JULIA *hurries off to the right*, JEAN *follows her eagerly*.]

THE PEASANTS *enter, led by a fiddler. They are in holiday clothes, with flowers in their hats. They have a barrel of small-ale and a keg of rough brandy, both wreathed with leaves, that they put on the table. They fetch glasses, and, when they have drunk, they take hands and dance round in a circle, singing* 'A lady walked in the wood . . .' *At the end, they dance out still singing.*

MISS JULIA *comes in alone. When she first sees the disorder in the kitchen, she clasps her hands. Then she takes out a powder puff and powders her face.*

JEAN [*entering – exultant*]: There, you see? And you've heard for yourself now – do you still think we can stay here now?

MISS JULIA: No, you're right – but what are we to do?

JEAN: Run away. Travel abroad – far from here.

MISS JULIA: Abroad? But where?

JEAN: Switzerland – or the Italian Lakes – you've never been there?

MISS JULIA: No, is it beautiful there?

JEAN: It's always summer – orange trees – laurels . . . ah!

MISS JULIA: But what should we do there?

JEAN: I'll start a hotel – a good one, for high-class visitors.

MISS JULIA: A hotel?

JEAN: Yes, There's a life for you! New faces all the time – new languages – no time to brood or get irritable – no wondering what to do next, there's always a job to hand: night and day there are bells to answer, trains to meet, and buses coming and going, and the gold rolling into the till all the time. Yes, there's a life for you!

MISS JULIA: A life for *you*, but what about me?

JEAN: But you'd be the mistress of the house – you'd be a great asset to the firm with your looks and your style. Why, we couldn't fail – not possibly! You'd sit in the office like a queen, and one touch on the electric bell'd bring all your slaves running. The visitors would file past your throne, and timidly lay their wealth on your desk – you've no idea how meek people are when they have a bill in their hands. And I'd cook the bills, too, and you'd sugar them with your sweetest smiles. Yes, let's get away from here – [*he pulls a time-table from his pocket*] now – by the next train. Yes, we could be in Malmö by 6.30, Hamburg by 8.40 tomorrow. Frankfort – and on to Basle the same day, then by the St Gothard to Como in – let's see – three days. Only three days!

MISS JULIA: It sounds wonderful. But you must give me the courage, Jean – put your arms round me and say you love me.

JEAN [*hesitantly*]: I'd like to, but I daren't – not in this house, not again. I do love you, though – truly – you believe that, don't you, Miss Julia?

MISS JULIA [*with becoming shyness*]: 'Miss'? Call me Julia. There are no barriers between us now. Call me Julia.

JEAN [*troubled*]: I can't. There'll always be barriers between us as long as we're in this house; I can't forget what I've been. And there's the Count – I've never met anyone I respect like him. I've only got to see his gloves on a chair, and I feel small; if his bell up there rings, I jump like a frightened horse. Why, when I look at his boots standing there, all stiff and proud, I feel I want to bow and scrape. [*He kicks the boots over.*] It's nothing but superstition – a tradition that's been dinned into us from childhood – it takes time to get over that. But if you'll only come abroad – to a country where there's a republic, and then they'll bow and scrape to my porters' livery – they shall go on their knees, you'll see. But *I* won't, I'm not meant for that sort of thing, I've got more in me – I've got character; and once I get hold of that first branch, you'll see me climb right to the top. I'm a servant now, but by next year I'll own a hotel; in ten years, I'll make enough to retire. Then I'll go to Rumania, and I'll let them pin decorations on me, and I may – mind you, I say *may* – finish up as a Count.

MISS JULIA: Good – good!

JEAN: Yes, you can buy a title in Rumania – so you'll be a Countess after all – *my* Countess.

MISS JULIA: What do I care about that? I'm finished with all that sort of thing – only tell me you love me, then I don't care what I am.

JEAN: I'll tell you so all day – later on, but not here. It's most important that we don't get sentimental, or we shall spoil everything. We must do it all cold-bloodedly, like sensible people. [*He takes a cigar, cuts the end, and lights it.*] Now you sit there, and I'll sit here, then we can talk it over just as if nothing had happened.

MISS JULIA [*desperately*]: My God, how can you be so callous!

JEAN: Me? Nobody's more soft-hearted than me – only I've got self-control, that's all.

MISS JULIA: And a little while ago you could kiss my shoe!

JEAN [*brusquely*]: A little while ago, yes; we've got something else to think about now.

MISS JULIA: How can you be so cruel?

JEAN: It's only common sense. We've made fools of ourselves once, why do it again? The Count may come back at any moment now – we've got to settle everything before he comes. Now, what do you think of my plans – do you agree?

MISS JULIA: They seem all right. There's only one thing: a big venture like that'd need a lot of capital – have you got it?

JEAN [*biting his cigar*]: Me? Of course I have; I'm a skilled man; I've got my years of experience, and my languages. The way I look at it, that's the sort of capital that counts.

MISS JULIA: But it won't buy you a railway ticket.

JEAN: That's true – that's why I need a backer who can put up the money.

MISS JULIA: Where will you find one – at such short notice?

JEAN: I leave that to you – if you want to come in with me.

MISS JULIA: But I can't, I haven't a penny of my own.

JEAN [*after a pause*]: Then it's all off.

MISS JULIA: But . . . ?

JEAN: We're back where we were.

MISS JULIA: Do you think I'm going to stay in this house as your mistress? And have them all whispering behind my back. How could I look my father in the face after this? No – take me away – I couldn't bear the scandal. Oh, God, what have I done? Oh God – Oh God!

[*She bursts into tears.*]

JEAN: Oh, so you're going to take that line, are you. What *have* you done? No more than plenty of other girls.

MISS JULIA: So you despise me now. [*Screaming hysterically*] I'm falling, I'm falling!

JEAN: Fall to my level, then, and I'll lift you up again.

MISS JULIA: What devil made me think you were attractive? Was it the attraction the weak feel for the strong – those who fall feel for those who are rising? Or was it love? Was *that* love? Do you know what love is?

JEAN: Me? You can take my word for it! – do you think I've never been there before?

MISS JULIA: That's no way to talk – you have a vulgar mind.

JEAN: That's the way I've been brought up – you must take me as I am. Now don't lose your head, and don't play the fine lady with me – we're in the same boat now. Come on, my girl, and I'll treat you to something special.

[*Opening the drawer, he takes out the bottle of wine, and fills the two used glasses.*]

MISS JULIA: Where did you get that wine?

JEAN: The cellar.

MISS JULIA: My father's Burgundy.

JEAN: Well, can't his son-in-law drink it?

MISS JULIA: And *I'm* drinking beer!

JEAN: That only shows your tastes are lower than mine.

MISS JULIA: Thief!

JEAN: Are you going to start a hue and cry?

MISS JULIA: Oh! I've thrown in my lot with a thief! I must have been drunk – or walking in my sleep! On Midsummer Eve, the night of innocent fun –

JEAN: Innocent? Well!

MISS JULIA [*pacing up and down*]: Oh, was anyone on earth ever so miserable as I am now!

JEAN: What have you got to be miserable about? You've done very well for yourself. What about Kristin – how d'you think she'd feel?

MISS JULIA: I used to think servants had feelings, now I know they haven't; a servant's a servant.

JEAN: And a whore's a whore!

MISS JULIA [*falling on her knees and clasping her hands*]: Oh, God in Heaven, take my wretched life – lift me out of the filth I'm sinking into. Save me – oh, save me!

JEAN: I don't mind admitting I feel sorry for you. When I lay in the onion bed, that time, and saw you in the rose-garden, I tell you straight, I had the same dirty ideas as other boys.

MISS JULIA: And then you wanted to die for me?

JEAN: In the oat-bin? Oh, that was all talk.

MISS JULIA: Do you mean it was a lie?

JEAN [*beginning to feel sleepy*]: More or less. I once read something of the sort in a paper: a chimney-sweep who shut himself in a chest full of elder-flowers – because he couldn't pay a maintenance order!

MISS JULIA: So that's the sort of man you are!

JEAN: Well, I had to think of something; women like that sort of talk.

MISS JULIA: Brute!

JEAN: *Merde!*

MISS JULIA: And now you've seen the back of the hawk!

JEAN: Well, not exactly its *back*!

MISS JULIA: So I had to be your lowest branch, did I?

JEAN: And the branch turned out to be rotten.

MISS JULIA: I'm to be the sign-board of your hotel –

JEAN: I'm the hotel, though.

MISS JULIA: – to sit in your office, attract your customers, and fake your bills.

JEAN: No, I'll see to that myself.

MISS JULIA: To think that a man could sink so low.

JEAN: You speak for yourself!

MISS JULIA: You servant! Lackey! Stand up when I speak to you!

JEAN: You servant's tart, you slut – shut your mouth and get out of here. You're a nice one to come nagging me about coarseness; no girl in my walk of life'd have made herself as cheap as you did tonight. Why even the meanest skivvy wouldn't throw herself at a man that way. Did you ever see a girl of *my* class carry on like that? I've never seen the like – except in the farmyard – or on the streets.

MISS JULIA [*crushed*]: That's right, hit me – trample on me – it's all I deserve – I'm dirt. But help me – help me out of it – if there is a way out!

JEAN [*more gently*]: I don't mind admitting my share of the honour of having seduced you – but do you think anyone in my position would have dared to as much as look at you unless *you* invited him? Why, even now I'm still amazed –

MISS JULIA: – and proud!

JEAN: Well, why not? All the same, you were too easy to be really exciting.

MISS JULIA: Yes – hit me – hit me!

JEAN [rising]: No, I shouldn't have said that – I'm sorry. I don't hit anyone when they're down – least of all a lady. All the same, I'm glad I've found out that what dazzles us underlings is only tinsel, and the fine complexion's powder, and the polished nails are black-edged – and the handkerchief may be dirty in spite of its perfume. Still, I'm sorry to find that what I was striving for wasn't truer – more worth-while. It hurts me to see you fall so much lower than your own cook; it's like seeing the flowers beaten down into the mud by the autumn rains.

MISS JULIA: You talk as though you'd already risen above me!

JEAN: So I have. Don't you see, I could make you a Countess – you could never make me a Count.

MISS JULIA: I'm the child of a Count, which is more than you could ever be.

JEAN: That's right – but I might be the father of Counts, if . . .

MISS JULIA: But you're a thief – I'm not.

JEAN: There are worse things than being a thief – much worse. Besides, when I'm working in a house, I look on myself almost like part of the family – one of the children, almost. You don't call it thieving if the children pick a little fruit when the bushes are heavy with it. [With reawakening passion]: Miss Julia – you're a fine woman – much too good for the likes of me. You lost your head and were swept off your feet, and now you want to put things right by persuading yourself you were in love with me. But you weren't. You may have been attracted by my looks – if that's all, then your love's no better than mine. If all you wanted was the animal in me, that'd never do for me – when I can't get your *love*.

MISS JULIA: Are you sure of that?

JEAN: D'you mean that perhaps . . .? I could love you, yes, I certainly could. You're beautiful, refined – [*He goes to her and takes her hand*] elegant – charming when you want to be. If you once set a man's heart on fire, it wouldn't be likely to go out. [*Putting his arm round her waist*] You're like hot wine with spices, and one kiss from you. . . .

[*He tries to lead her away, but she gently frees herself.*]

MISS JULIA: Let go of me – that's not the way to win me.

JEAN: Then how? 'That's not the way', eh? If you don't want kisses and pretty speeches – or someone who'll plan for you, and save you from degrading yourself – then how?

MISS JULIA: I don't know how; I've no idea. I hate you – as I'd hate a rat. But I can't free myself from you.

JEAN: Come away with me.

MISS JULIA [*straightening her dress*]: Away? Yes, of course, we'll run away. But I'm tired – give me a glass of wine. [*While* JEAN *pours it out, she looks at her watch.*] We must talk things over first – there's still time.

[*She empties her glass and holds it out for more.*]

JEAN: Don't drink so much, it'll go to your head.

MISS JULIA: What does it matter?

JEAN: What does it matter? It's vulgar to get drunk. What were you going to say?

MISS JULIA: We'll run away; but we must talk it over first. At least *I* must – so far *you've* done all the talking. You've told me all about your life – now I'm going to tell you mine. Then we'll know all about each other before we start on our travels together.

JEAN: Just a minute. Look, excuse me – but think it over before you tell me any secrets you'll be sorry for later.

MISS JULIA: Aren't you my friend?

JEAN: For the moment – but don't rely on me.

MISS JULIA: You don't mean that. Anyhow, everybody knows my secrets. My mother wasn't a noblewoman – her people were quite ordinary. She was brought up according to all the theories of her time about the equality and freedom of women and all that. She could never bear the thought of marriage; when my father proposed she swore that she would never be his wife, but she married him in the end. As far as I can make out, I was born against her wishes. Then she wanted to bring me up to lead what she used to call 'a child's natural life'; I was to learn everything a boy does – just to prove that a woman's as good as a man. I had to wear boy's clothes, and learn how to handle a horse – though I wasn't allowed in the dairy. I had to groom the horses, and harness them, and hunt; I even had to try to learn farm work. On our estate, the men were given women's work and the women men's – till everything went to pieces, and we were the laughing-stock of the whole neighbourhood. At last my father seemed to have woken up from his trance; he asserted himself at last, and things were run his way. My mother became ill; I don't know what was the matter with her, but she kept having convulsions. She used to hide herself in the attics or out in the grounds – sometimes she'd stay out all night. Then came the big fire – you must have heard about it. The house and the stables and the barns were all burnt down, and in a way that made it look as if it were started on purpose, because it happened the very day after the insurance expired, and the new premium that my father had sent was delayed through the messenger going astray, so it got there too late.

[*She fills her glass and drinks.*]

JEAN: Don't drink any more.

MISS JULIA: Oh, what does it matter? . . . We hadn't a roof over our heads, and we had to sleep in the carriages. My father didn't know where to get the money to rebuild. Then my mother advised him to try to borrow it from a friend she'd known all her life – a brick-manufacturer not far from here. My father got the loan – and to his great surprise, without any interest; so the house was rebuilt. [*She drinks again.*] Do you know who started the fire?

JEAN: Her ladyship – your mother.

MISS JULIA: And who do you think the brick-manufacturer was?

JEAN: Your mother's lover.

MISS JULIA: Do you know whose money it was?

JEAN: Wait a minute. . . . No, I don't know that.

MISS JULIA: It was my mother's.

JEAN: In other words, the Count's — unless their estates were separate.

MISS JULIA: They were. My mother had some money of her own that she wouldn't let my father touch; she'd invested it — with the friend.

JEAN: . . . Who pinched it?

MISS JULIA: Exactly — he kept it. My father found out. He couldn't pay his wife's lover, he couldn't prove it was his wife's money. That was my mother's revenge, because he'd made himself master in his own house. For a time he felt like shooting himself — as a matter of fact, they say he tried to, and failed. Well, in the end, he lived it down and made my mother pay for what she'd done. You can guess what those first years were like for me! I was sorry for my father, but I sided with my mother — you see, I didn't know the true story then. She taught me to mistrust and hate men — I expect you've heard she hated the whole sex— and I swore to her that I'd never be a slave to any man.

JEAN: Yet you were engaged to the County Attorney.

MISS JULIA: Only to make him *my* slave.

JEAN: And he wouldn't be.

MISS JULIA: Oh, he would have been all right, if I'd let him, but I got tired of him.

JEAN: So I saw — in the stable-yard.

MISS JULIA: What did you see?

JEAN: That's what I saw! How he broke off the engagement.

MISS JULIA: That's a lie — *I* broke it off. Did he say he broke it? — The brute!

JEAN: I'm not so sure he was a brute. So you hate men, Miss Julia.

MISS JULIA: I do . . . but there are times when a woman is weak . . . and then . . .

JEAN: Do you hate me?

MISS JULIA: More than I can say! I'd willingly shoot you like an animal –

JEAN: – quick as a flash – the way they shoot a mad dog, eh?

MISS JULIA: Exactly.

JEAN: But you haven't got a gun – and there isn't a dog here – so what are we to do?

MISS JULIA: Go abroad . . .

JEAN: – and make life hell for each other for the rest of our days?

MISS JULIA: No, to enjoy ourselves. For a few days – a week – as long as we can – and then die.

JEAN: Die? That's silly. If you ask me, it'd be better to start the hotel.

MISS JULIA [without listening to JEAN]: By Lake Como, where the sun's always shining, and the oranges shine on the trees, and the laurels have fresh green leaves at Christmas-time.

JEAN: Lake Como is a rainy hole, and I never saw any oranges there except on fruit stalls. But it's full of tourists, and there are plenty of villas to rent to loving couples, and that's a paying game – you know why? Because they take a six months' lease, and then leave after three weeks.

MISS JULIA [naïvely]: Why after three weeks?

JEAN: Because they quarrel, of course. But they have to pay the rent just the same. Then you let the house again, and so it goes on; there's always plenty of lovers, even though they don't last.

MISS JULIA: Then you don't want to die with me.

JEAN: I don't want to die at all; I enjoy life. Besides, I think suicide's a sin against my Maker who gave us our life.

MISS JULIA: Do you mean to say *you* believe in God?

JEAN: Of course I do. And I go to church every other Sunday. Look, to tell you the truth, I'm tired of all this – I'm off to bed.

MISS JULIA: Oh, *are* you! Do you think I'm going to be content with that? Don't you know a man owes a woman something when he's dishonoured her?

JEAN [*taking out his purse and throwing a silver piece on the table*]: You're welcome! I'm sure I don't want to be in anyone's debt.

MISS JULIA [*pretending to ignore the insult*]: You know the legal penalty – ?

JEAN: Too bad there's no legal penalty for a woman who seduces a man!

MISS JULIA: What else is there for us but to go abroad – marry and then separate?

JEAN: And suppose I won't take on such a bad match.

MISS JULIA: A bad match?

JEAN: Yes, for me. My stock's better than yours – no one in my family ever committed arson.

MISS JULIA: How do you know?

JEAN: You can't prove otherwise, since we haven't any pedigree – except in the Parish records. But I've seen your family tree in a book on the drawing-room table. D'you know who founded your family? A miller, who let the king sleep with his wife one night in the Danish war. I haven't got that sort of ancestor, but I can found a family myself.

MISS JULIA: This is what I get for giving my heart to a wretch like you – for sacrificing my family honour –

JEAN: *Dishonour*. Well, I warned you; I told you not to drink or you'd say something you'd be sorry for. It doesn't do to talk too much.

MISS JULIA: Oh, I wish it hadn't happened – what can have made me do it? If only you *loved* me!

JEAN: Oh, for the last time – what do you expect me to do? Burst into tears? Jump over your hunting crop? Kiss you, and lure you down to Lake Como for three weeks – and all the rest of it? What do you expect? I've had just about enough of this – it's always the way if you get mixed up with women. Now look, Miss Julia – I can see you're unhappy, I know what you're going through – but I can't understand you. *We* never carry on like this; we don't hate each other. With us, love's just a game – something to do in our time off; we haven't got all day and all night for it, like you. I believe you're ill – yes that's it, you must be ill.

MISS JULIA: Oh, talk kindly to me – be human.

JEAN: You be human yourself, then; if you spit on me, you must expect me to wipe it off on you.

MISS JULIA: Help me – help me. Just tell me what to do – how to get out of this.

JEAN: Good God, if only I knew myself!

MISS JULIA: I've been a fool – out of my mind – but isn't there *some* way out?

JEAN: Stay here and keep your mouth shut – no one knows.

MISS JULIA: But they must! The farm people know – and Kristin knows.

JEAN: They don't know; and anyhow they'd never believe it.

MISS JULIA [*slowly*]: But – but it might happen again.

JEAN: That's true.

MISS JULIA: And – the consequences?

JEAN [*frightened*]: The consequences! What a fool I was not to think of that! Well, there's only one thing to do – you must clear out – at once. I can't go with you, that would ruin everything; you must go by yourself – abroad – anywhere you like.

MISS JULIA: Alone? Where? *I can't!*

JEAN: You must. Before the Count comes back too. You know what'll happen if you stay: after the first step – well, the damage is done, so why not carry on! Then you get a bit careless – till in the end you're caught! No, you must get away. Then write to the Count and confess. Only don't go and mention my name – he'd never guess – I don't expect he'd be too keen to find out, anyway.

MISS JULIA: I'll go if you'll come too.

JEAN: Are you off your head, woman? Miss Julia running away
with her footman? It'd be in all the papers the next day, and
that'd finish the Count.

MISS JULIA: I can't go – I can't stay. Help me, I'm so tired – so
terribly tired. Order me! That would start me off, but I can't
do anything for myself – I can't even think any more.

JEAN: Now you see what you gentry are worth. Why should you
strut about and turn up your noses as if you were the lords of
creation? All right, you can take orders from me. Go up and
get dressed – get some money for the journey – and then come
down here.

MISS JULIA [half-whispering]: Come up with me!

JEAN: To your room? You're crazy! [He hesitates a moment.] No –
get out. Quick.

[He takes her by the hand and pulls her to the door.]

MISS JULIA [as she goes]: You might speak nicely to me, Jean.

JEAN: An order always sounds cruel – now you know what it
feels like.

[JEAN, left alone, with a sigh of relief, sits at the table and takes
out a notebook and pencil. Every now and then he reckons up aloud;
apart from that, he continues in dumbshow till KRISTIN comes in,
dressed for church. She has a white tie and a shirt-front in her hand.]

KRISTIN: Good Lord, what a mess the place is in – what have you
been up to?

JEAN: Oh, Miss Julia dragged a whole crowd in. You must have
slept soundly – didn't you hear anything?

KRISTIN: I slept like a log.

JEAN: And you're dressed for church already!

KRISTIN: Yes – didn't you promise to go to Communion with
me?

JEAN: Oh, yes, so I did. And you've brought my things. Give
me a hand with them. [He sits down. There is a pause, while
KRISTIN helps him on with the false front and the tie.]

JEAN [sleepily]: What's the lesson for today?

KRISTIN: The beheading of John the Baptist, I think.

JEAN: Oh, that'll go on for hours. Look out, you're choking me. Oh Lord, I'm sleepy!

KRISTIN: What have you been doing, up all night? You look ready to drop!

JEAN: I've been sitting here talking with Miss Julia.

KRISTIN: She doesn't know how to behave, *that* she doesn't!

JEAN [*pause*]: Look – Kristin –

KRISTIN: Well?

JEAN: It's funny when you come to think of it. . . Her!

KRISTIN: What's so funny?

JEAN: The whole thing. [*Pause.*]

KRISTIN [*looking at the half-empty glasses on the table*]: And have you been drinking together, too?

JEAN: Yes.

KRISTIN: For shame! Look me in the face.

JEAN: Yes.

KRISTIN: Oh, how could you! How could you?

JEAN [*after a moment*]: Well, there it is.

KRISTIN: Faugh, I'd never have thought it, *that* I wouldn't. Oh, for shame!

JEAN: You don't mean to say you're jealous of her?

KRISTIN: Not of her, no; if it had been Clara or Sophie I'd have scratched your eyes out. I don't know why, but that's the way it is. No, this really was disgusting!

JEAN: You're angry with her, then?

KRISTIN: I'm angry with you. Oh, it was wicked of you, downright wicked. That poor girl. I tell you, I'm not stopping here another day – not in a house where you can't respect your betters.

JEAN: Why should you respect them?

KRISTIN: Yes, you may well ask that, Mr Clever. But you wouldn't go working for people who don't know how to behave. It'd be degrading if you ask *me*!

JEAN: You ought to be proud to know they're no better than us.

KRISTIN: Well, I'm not. What's the use of trying to better

yourself if they're no better after all? Besides, what about the Count? Think of all he's had to put up with in his time! No, I don't stay in this house another day. And with a fellow like you, too! If it had been the County Attorney — someone a bit better —

JEAN: Here, wait a minute —

KRISTIN: Oh, you're all right in your way, but class is class all the same; that's a thing I never forget. My Lady was always so proud, too; so off-hand with men, that you'd never think she'd go and give herself . . . and to a man like you! Why, she wanted to have poor Diana shot for going with the porter's mongrel! Well, there it is. I'm not staying here — on the 24th of October, I leave.

JEAN: And then?

KRISTIN: Yes, come to think of it, it's high time you looked for another place, too, since we're going to get married.

JEAN: But what kind of work? I couldn't get a place like this if I was married.

KRISTIN: Of course not, but you could get a job as a porter — or a commissionaire in some Government building. You won't get fat on Government pay, but it's regular — and there's a pension for the widow and children.

JEAN [with a wry face]: That's all very fine, but I've no intention of dying for my wife and children just yet. I don't mind telling you I've got a little more ambition than that.

KRISTIN: You may have ambition, but you've got your duty too, and don't you forget it.

JEAN: I know all about my duty without you nagging me. [He is listening for something off-stage.] Still, we've got plenty of time to think about that later. Go and get ready, and then we'll go to church.

KRISTIN: Who's that moving about upstairs?

JEAN: I don't know — probably Clara.

KRISTIN [going]: Do you think the Count could have come home without us hearing him?

JEAN [*frightened*]: The Count? No, it couldn't be, he'd have rung.

KRISTIN [*as she goes*]: God help us! I've never seen the like of this.

[*The sun has risen now*] *lighting the tops of the trees in the park. The light moves gradually, till it slants through the window.* JEAN *goes to the door and makes a sign.*]

MISS JULIA [*comes in; she is in travelling clothes, and carries a small birdcage, covered with a napkin, which she puts on a chair*]: I'm all ready.

JEAN: Ssh, Kristin's awake.

MISS JULIA [*she is extremely nervous throughout this scene*]: Does she suspect?

JEAN: Not a thing. My God, you look a sight.

MISS JULIA: Why, what's the matter?

JEAN: You're as pale as a ghost – and if you don't mind me saying so, your face is dirty.

MISS JULIA: Let me wash it, then. Here. [*She goes to the basin and washes her face and hands.*] Give me a towel. Oh, there's the sun!

JEAN: And all the goblins vanish!

MISS JULIA: Yes, there were certainly goblins about last night. Listen Jean, come with me; I've got the money now.

JEAN [*doubtfully*]: Enough?

MISS JULIA: Enough to start with. Come with me, I can't travel alone today. Think of it – Midsummer Day in a stuffy train, jammed in with a lot of staring people; stuck in stations when you're longing to be moving. . . . No, I can't do it, I can't. I should remember other Midsummer Days – Midsummer Days when I was a child, and the church was all hung with birch and lilac; the dinner-table decorated for all our friends and relations; music and dancing in the park after dinner, and flowers and games. Oh, however far you run away, your memories follow in the luggage van – and regret and remorse, too!

JEAN: I'll come with you – but now, at once, before it's too late. We must go this minute.

MISS JULIA: Get ready, then.

[*She picks up the cage.*]

JEAN: No luggage, though – that'd only give us away.

MISS JULIA: No, no luggage – only what we can take in the compartment with us.

JEAN [*fetching his hat*]: What's that? What on earth have you got there?

MISS JULIA: Only my greenfinch, I couldn't bear to leave him behind.

JEAN: Oh, for goodness sake! Have we got to drag a birdcage round with us? You're off your head. Put it down.

MISS JULIA: He's the only thing I want to take; he's the only living creature that loves me, now Diana's deserted me. Don't be so cruel – let me take him with me!

JEAN: Put it down, I tell you. And don't talk so loud or Kristin'll hear.

MISS JULIA: I can't leave him here with no one to look after him; I'd rather you killed him.

JEAN: All right, give me the little beast, I'll wring its neck.

MISS JULIA: Don't hurt him, will you? Don't – Oh, I can't!

JEAN: Well, I can – let's have it.

[*She takes the bird out of the cage and kisses it.*]

MISS JULIA: My poor little Greenie! Have you got to die because of your mistress, then?

JEAN: Oh, for goodness sake don't make a scene: your whole future's in the balance – the rest of your life. Hurry up! [*He snatches the bird from her, and, picking up a chopper, takes it over to the block. MISS JULIA turns away.*] You ought to have learnt to kill chickens, instead of revolver-shooting . . . [*brings down the chopper*] – then you wouldn't faint at a drop of blood.

MISS JULIA [*shrieking*]: Kill me – kill me too, if you can kill an innocent creature like that without turning a hair. I hate you!

Now I hate you! There's blood between us! I wish to God I'd never seen you — I wish to God I'd never been born.

MISS JULIA [*going to the chopping-block as if she were drawn there against her will*]: No, I won't go yet — I can't — I must see. Hush, there's a carriage outside . . . [*She seems to listen, but she never takes her eyes from the block and the chopper.*] So you think I can't stand the sight of blood? You think I'm so weak? How I'd love to see your blood, and your brains, on a chopping-block! I'd like to see your whole sex swimming in a sea of blood, like this creature here. I think I could drink out of your skull, dabble my feet in your chest, and eat your heart roasted whole. You think I'm weak; you think I love you, just because something in me cried out for your seed! Do you think I want to carry your spawn under my heart, and nourish it with my blood — bear your child and take your name? Incidentally, what *is* your name? I've never heard your surname — if you've got one. I'm to be Mrs Doorkeeper or Madame Dustheap, I suppose! You dog, with my collar round your neck, you lackey with my crest on your buttons; I'm to share you with my cook, am I, and be the rival of my own servant? Oh . . . h! You think I'm a coward — you think I'll run away! No, I'm staying here, even if the heavens fall! My father'll come home, he'll find his desk broken open and his money gone. Then he'll ring — that bell there — two rings for the footman. Then he'll send for the police, and I shall tell him everything — everything! And thank God that'll be the end of it — if there *is* an end. He'll have a stroke and die, and that'll be the finish of all of us. And then there'll be peace — quiet — everlasting rest. They'll break his escutcheon over his coffin, his noble line'll be extinct. But the lackey's stock will go on — in a foundling hospital — he'll win his spurs in the gutter, and end in a gaol.

JEAN: There's the royal blood speaking — well done, my lady! Cram the miller back in his sack.

[KRISTIN *comes in, dressed for church, with a hymn-book in her hand.*]

MISS JULIA [*running to her arms, as if for protection*]: Help me! Help me against this man!

KRISTIN [*cold and unmoved*]: This is a pretty sight for a Sunday morning. [*She sees the chopping-block.*] And what's all this mess you've made here? What does it all mean – all this shouting and screaming?

MISS JULIA: Kristin, you're a woman, you're my friend. Don't trust this man, he's a scoundrel.

JEAN [*somewhat shamefacedly*]: If you ladies are going to argue the point, I'll go and shave.

[*He slips out to the right.*]

MISS JULIA: Listen to me, Kristin, you must listen – *you*'ll understand.

KRISTIN: I certainly don't understand this sort of behaviour! And where are you off to – you're dressed for a journey, and he had his hat on? What does it all mean?

MISS JULIA: Listen, Kristin, listen to me and I'll tell you everything.

KRISTIN: I don't want to hear anything about it.

MISS JULIA: You *must* listen.

KRISTIN: What is it, then? – Do you mean your carrying on with Jean? That doesn't worry me, it's none of my business. But if you're planning to take him away with you, I'll soon put paid to that!

MISS JULIA [*overwrought*]: Try to be reasonable, Kristin, and listen to me. I can't stay here – neither can Jean – so we must go abroad.

KRISTIN: Oho?

MISS JULIA [*suddenly*]: Here's an idea, though; suppose we all three go – abroad – to Switzerland. We'll start a hotel together, I've got money. Jean and I'll look after everything, and I thought you'd take over the kitchen. Wouldn't that be fine? Say you'll come, then that'll settle everything. Do say you'll come, dear Kristin.

[*She throws her arms round Kristin and strokes her.*]

KRISTIN [*receiving the idea coolly*]: Well . . .

MISS JULIA [*urgently*]: You've never been abroad, Kristin – you ought to get out and see the world. You've no idea what fun it is, travelling by train – always seeing new people – new countries. When we get to Hamburg, we'll go to the zoo on our way through – you'll enjoy that; and we'll go to theatres and the Opera. And when we get to Munich, there'll be the museums: there are Raphaels and Rubens – the great painters, you know. You've heard of Munich, where King Ludwig lived – the king who went mad, you know; we'll go over his castles – there are still castles of his, furnished like a fairy-tale. And it's not far from there to Switzerland – and the Alps – think of the Alps, with snow on them in mid-summer; and oranges grow there, and laurels that are green all the year round. . . . [JEAN *is visible in the wings at the right; he is stropping his razor, holding the strap between his teeth and his left hand. He listens with amusement to what she says, now and then nodding approval. Still more urgently*]: And then we'll have a hotel – I shall sit in the office, while Jean stands and receives the guests, does the shopping, writes letters. There's a life for you! Trains to meet, and buses calling, bells to answer – upstairs and down in the restaurant – I'd make out the bills – I know how to cook them too. You've no idea how meek travellers are when it comes to paying bills. And you – you'll sit and run the kitchen – no standing at the stove, of course. You'll have to dress smartly, when you meet the visitors – you with your looks – no, I mean it – you'll soon get yourself a husband – a rich Englishman, probably – they're easy to catch. [*Getting slower*]: And then we'll get rich, and we'll build a villa on Lake Como; . . . of course it rains there now and then, [*dully*] . . . but there's sure to be sunshine too, even if there *are* clouds. And then. . . . Then we can come home again . . . here . . . or somewhere else –

KRISTIN: Now listen, Miss, do you really believe all that?

MISS JULIA [*crushed*]: Do I believe – ?

KRISTIN: Yes.

MISS JULIA: I don't know — I don't believe anything any longer. [*She sinks down on the bench, and drops her head on to her arms as they lie on the table.*] Nothing — nothing at all.

KRISTIN [*looking to the right where* JEAN *is standing*]: Well, well, so you are going to run away?

JEAN [*shamefacedly, putting his razor on the table*]: Run away? Well, I wouldn't put it like that. You heard what Miss Julia suggests; she's tired now, because she's been up all night, but it's a good scheme and it might work.

KRISTIN: Now you listen to me! If you think I'm going to cook for that . . .

JEAN: You keep a civil tongue in your head when you talk about your mistress — d'you hear?

KRISTIN: Mistress!

JEAN: Yes, mistress.

KRISTIN: Well, well, listen to him!

JEAN: You'd better listen yourself for a change, and don't talk so much. Miss Julia's your mistress. And if it comes to that, who are *you* to turn up your nose at her for what she did?

KRISTIN: I've got too much self-respect to —

JEAN: — to be able to respect anyone else!

KRISTIN: — to go below my station! You can't say the Count's cook ever had anything to do with the groom or the swineherd; you can't say that.

JEAN: No, you got yourself a nice steady chap — lucky for you.

KRISTIN: So steady that he sells the oats from the Count's stable.

JEAN: Who are *you* to talk? You get a commission on the groceries, to say nothing of bribes from the butcher.

KRISTIN: I don't know what you mean!

JEAN: So you can't respect your mistress any more! *You* indeed!

KRISTIN: Are you coming to church with me? After what you've been up to, you need a good sermon.

JEAN: No, I'm not going to church today. You go by yourself and confess your sins.

KRISTIN: All right, I will, and I'll bring back enough forgiveness for you, too. Our Lord suffered and died on the Cross for our sins, and if we go to Him with faith and a contrite heart, He will take all our guilt on Himself.

MISS JULIA: Do you believe that, Kristin?

KRISTIN: I've believed it all my life, as sure as I stand here. I learnt it when I was little, and I've always believed it, Miss Julia. 'Where sin aboundeth, there grace aboundeth also.'

MISS JULIA: If only I had your faith – if only –

KRISTIN: That doesn't come without God's special grace, and that isn't given to everyone –

MISS JULIA: Who has it, then?

KRISTIN: That's the great secret of the Kingdom of Heaven, Miss Julia. God is no respector of persons; the Last shall be First –

MISS JULIA: Then He must respect the Last.

KRISTIN [continuing]: – It is easier for a camel to pass through a needle's eye, than for a rich man to enter the Kingdom of Heaven. Yes, that's how it is, Miss Julia. Well, I'm going now, by myself. And on my way, I'll tell the stable-boy not to let any horses out, in case anyone should want to get away before the Count comes back. Goodbye.

[She goes.]

JEAN: What a spitfire! And all because of a wretched bird!

MISS JULIA [dully]: Never mind the bird. Can you see any way out of this? Any end to it?

JEAN [thinking]: I can't.

MISS JULIA: What would you do in my place?

JEAN: In your place? Let me think. . . . A woman of your class, who's gone wrong. . . . I don't know. Yes, I do, though.

MISS JULIA [she picks up the razor, and makes a significant gesture]: Like this?

JEAN: Yes. But I wouldn't do it, mind you – that's the difference between us.

MISS JULIA: Because you're a man and I'm a woman? What difference does that make?

JEAN: Just the difference that there *is* between man and woman.

MISS JULIA [*with the razor in her hand*]: I wish I could. . . . I can't do it, though – any more than my father could – that time when he should have done it.

JEAN: No, he shouldn't: he had to have his revenge first.

MISS JULIA: And now my mother gets *her* revenge – through me.

JEAN: Haven't you ever loved your father, Miss Julia?

MISS JULIA: Yes – very much. But I must have hated him, too; I must have been hating him without realizing it. You see he taught me to despise my own sex – to be half woman and half man. Who's to blame for all this – my father, or my mother, or myself? Myself? I haven't a self; I haven't a thought that I don't get from my father, nor an emotion that I don't get from my mother. Even this last idea that all human beings are equal – that came from my fiancé – and then I call him a beast for his pains. How can I be to blame? Am I to put all the blame on Jesus, like Kristin? No, I'm too proud to do that – and too sensible, thanks to my father's teaching. As for the rich man not going to heaven, that's a lie; Kristin, with money in her savings bank, wouldn't get in. But who's to blame? Still, what does that matter? I'm the one who has to bear the blame and take the consequences.

JEAN: Yes, but – [*There are two sharp rings on the bell.* MISS JULIA *leaps to her feet –* JEAN *slips on his other coat.*] That's the Count – he's home! [*Going*] Suppose Kristin has . . .

[*He goes to the speaking-tube, taps on it, and listens.*]

MISS JULIA: Has he been to his desk yet?

JEAN: It's Jean, my lord. [*He listens, but the audience do not hear the Count's reply.*] Yes, my lord. [*Listens*] Yes, my lord, at once. [*Listens*] Very well, my lord – in half an hour.

MISS JULIA [*quite distraught*]: What did he say? Oh, God, what did he say?

JEAN: He wants his boots and his coffee in half an hour.

MISS JULIA: Half an hour! Oh, I'm so tired; I can't do anything: I can't repent, I can't run away, I can't stay; I can't live, I can't die. Help me now! Order me, and I'll obey you like a dog. Do this last thing for me: save my honour, save my name. You know what I ought to do if only I had the will-power. *Will* me to do it – and command me to obey you.

JEAN: I don't know – I can't, now, either – I don't know why. It's just as if this coat stopped me. I can't order you now – not since the Count spoke to me – I can't explain it, it must be this livery I've put on my back. I really believe if the Count were to come down here now and order me to cut my throat, I'd do it on the spot.

MISS JULIA: Then pretend you're the Count and I'm you! You could play the part quite well just now, when you were on your knees; you were the aristocrat then all right. Oh, haven't you ever seen a hypnotist on the stage? [JEAN *nods.*] He says to his subject, 'Take that broom', and he takes it. Then he says, 'Sweep', and he sweeps.

JEAN: He has to be in a trance, though.

MISS JULIA [*ecstatic*]: I'm asleep already. The whole room seems full of smoke – you look to me like an iron furnace – a furnace that's like a man dressed in black, with a tall hat. Your eyes are glowing like coals when the fire sinks down, and your face is a white blur like ashes. [*The sunlight has reached the floor, and is now falling on* JEAN.] Oh, it's warm and lovely – [*she rubs her hands together as if she were warming them at a fire*] and so light – and so peaceful.

JEAN [*taking the razor and putting it into her hand*]: That's your broom. It's daylight now – go out into the barn and . . . [*whispers in her ear.*]

MISS JULIA [*rousing herself*]: Thank you – now I'm going to have peace at last. But before I go, tell me that the First can receive the gift of grace, too. Say it, even if you don't believe it.

JEAN: The First can have . . . No, I can't say that! Wait, though,

Miss Julia, I've got it! You're not the First any longer – you're among the Last!

MISS JULIA: That's true; I'm among the very Last – I *am* the Last. Oh, but now I can't go. Tell me to go – tell me again!

JEAN: I can't either, now – I can't!

MISS JULIA: 'And the First shall be Last' –

JEAN: Don't think – don't think. You're taking away my strength and making me a coward. What's that! I thought the bell moved. No – let's stuff it with paper. Fancy being so afraid of a bell! Yes, but it's something more than just a bell – there's someone behind it – a hand that sets it moving – and something else that moves the hand. Stop your ears then – simply stop your ears! But then it rings more than ever; it rings and rings till you answer it – and then it's too late. The police come . . . and then . . . [*Two sharp rings from the bell.* JEAN *shrinks for a moment, and then straightens himself.*] It's horrible – but there's no other way out. Go . . .

[*With a firm step,* MISS JULIA *goes out through the door.*]

CURTAIN

EASTER

A PLAY IN THREE ACTS

(1901)

THIRTEEN years passed between *Miss Julia* and *Easter* – years filled with poverty, bitterness, illness, and disappointment. Now, Strindberg was slowly learning to come to terms with life. He had written the first two plays of his confessional trilogy, *To Damascus*, and had fallen in love with the young actress Harriet Bosse who had played 'The Lady' in them. It was for her that he wrote the part of Eleonora, in this, the most tender of his plays.

His unmarried sister Elizabeth was now in an asylum in Uppsala. Her mind had been failing since Strindberg's own Inferno period, and Strindberg felt that she had mystically taken all his sins on herself, and was suffering for them. He believed also that he was in telepathic contact with her while he was writing this play. It was round her, and his memories of her as a child, that he created the character of Eleonora – the innocent who suffers for others; and he named her after his beloved mother.

In this play we see memories of Strindberg's own youth: his father had gone bankrupt just before Strindberg was born; his childhood was haunted by creditors and the removal of the furniture must have been a continual threat.

In Elis he has drawn his own jealousy and stubborn arrogance, and has recalled his own feelings when he taught at the Klara school, remembering how, that winter over thirty years before, he had longed for the spring when he could put away his heavy, shabby overcoat. The idea that 'everything comes full circle' which pervades this play and others of this period, started from these teaching days. He was particularly sensitive to the coincidences in his life and he had some reason to be. His first post as a teacher was not in the country, as he had hoped, but in the dismal school where he had been so wretched as a pupil; and when he first met Siri von Essen, she and her husband were living in the very house where he had spent much of his unhappy childhood.

He has set the play in Lund, the little provincial town where he spent the winter of 1896 recuperating after his mental breakdown. Here he watched the spring return, and 'was moved as never before by the sufferings of Holy Week and the deliverance of Easter Sunday'.

In the last Act, Lindkvist dispels, one after the other, all the unworthy suspicions and hatreds that Elis has been cherishing for so long. It is almost as if Strindberg, who had suffered all his life from what to-day we should call a persecution complex, were exorcizing his own dark imaginings.

EASTER

CHARACTERS

MRS HEYST
ELIS, *her son, a teacher, with a
University degree*
ELEONORA, *her daughter*
KRISTINA, *Elis's fiancée*
BENJAMIN, *a schoolboy*
LINDKVIST

*The scene remains the same throughout the play. The whole fore-stage
represents a glass-fronted verandah on the ground floor, furnished as a
sitting-room. A large door in the centre leads to the garden, which has
a fence with a gate onto the street. Across the street (which, like the
house, is on a height) can be seen the low fence of a garden sloping
down towards the town. The backcloth shows the tree-tops of this garden,
in fresh spring leaf; farther away, a church tower and the tall gable of
a house are visible.*

*The glass windows of the verandah, which stretch the whole width
of the stage, are hung with flowered curtains of light yellow cretonne,
which can be drawn. On a window-frame to the left of the door hangs
a mirror, and, below it, a calendar.*

*To the right of this centre door is a large desk, with books, writing-
materials, and a telephone. To the left is a dining-table, a mica-fronted
stove, and a sideboard. Down-stage, right, is a work-table with a lamp,
and two armchairs beside it. A hanging lamp is suspended from the
ceiling.*

Out in the street is a lamp-post with an incandescent gas burner.

*A door in the left wall of the verandah leads to the other rooms; a
door to the right leads to the kitchen.*

The time is the present day (1901).

ACT ONE

MAUNDY THURSDAY

*[Before the curtain rises, Haydn's 'Seven Words from the Cross' Intro-
duction: Maestoso Adagio, should be played.*

*A sunbeam slants across the room from the right, and falls on one of
the chairs by the work-table. In the other chair, which is in the shadow,
sits* KRISTINA *threading a tape in a pair of freshly-ironed white muslin
curtains.* ELIS *comes in, wearing his winter overcoat unbuttoned, and
carrying a large bundle of documents which he puts on the desk before
going left to take off his overcoat and hang it up.]*

ELIS: Good afternoon, dear.

KRISTINA: Hullo, Elis.

ELIS *[looking round]*: The double windows down, the floor
scrubbed, and clean curtains! It's really spring again! They've
scraped up the ice off the street, and down by the river the
willows are out. Yes, it's spring. And I can put my winter
coat away. *[He weighs it in his hand.]* You know, it's as heavy as
if it had absorbed the whole winter's troubles, and all the
sweat and dust and worry of the classroom. Ah. . . .

KRISTINA: And now the holidays are here!

ELIS: The Easter holidays! Five glorious days to live and breathe
and forget. *[He holds out his hand to* KRISTINA, *and then sits
in the free chair.]* And just look, here's the sun again! I remember the day, back in November, when it disappeared behind
the brewery across the street. What a winter it's been – what
a long winter.

KRISTINA *[indicating the kitchen door]*: Sh! Sh!

ELIS: Yes, I must be quiet, and just be glad that it's over. Oh,
this lovely sun! *[He rubs his hands as if he were taking a shower.]*
I'd like to bathe in sunshine – wash myself all over in light,
after all this filthy darkness!

KRISTINA: Sh!

ELIS: Do you know, I believe our luck's turned, and we're going to have some peace again.

KRISTINA: What makes you think that?

ELIS: Well, for one thing, as I was passing the Cathedral just now, a white dove came flying down onto the pavement with a twig in its beak, and it dropped it right at my feet!

KRISTINA: What sort of a twig was it? Did you notice?

ELIS: Well, it couldn't very well have been olive, but I'm sure it was a token of peace, and already I can feel a heavenly, sunlit calm. Where's Mother?

KRISTINA [indicating the kitchen]: In the kitchen.

ELIS [quietly, closing his eyes]: Now I can *hear* that it's spring. I can hear that the double windows are down. Do you know how? Mostly because I can hear the cart-wheels, but – listen, there's a bullfinch starting to sing! Then there's the sound of hammering from the dockyard, and they're painting the steamers – I can smell the red lead.

KRISTINA: How can you smell that from so far away?

ELIS: So far? Yes, of course you're right, we're *here*. Just for the moment I was back in our home, away up in the north. Why did we ever come to this terrible town, where everyone hates everyone else, and it's always lonely? Of course we had to, to earn a living, but it only brought us bad luck – father's arrest, and little Eleonora's illness. . . . By the way, do you know if they've let Mother see him in prison yet?

KRISTINA: I believe she's been there today.

ELIS: What did she say?

KRISTINA: Nothing – she kept talking about other things.

ELIS: Well, there's one good thing. Once the trial was over, we knew where we were, and that was a relief, there was nothing more about it in the newspapers, either. Here's one year gone, and in another he'll be free, and we'll be able to make a fresh start.

KRISTINA: I think you're wonderful to be so patient about it.

ELIS: No, don't say that – there's nothing wonderful about me,

I have all kinds of faults. Now you know. I only wish you'd believe it.

KRISTINA: It isn't your own faults you're suffering for, it's someone else's.

ELIS: What are you making there?

KRISTINA: It's the kitchen curtains, dear.

ELIS: They look like a bridal veil. You will marry me this autumn, won't you?

KRISTINA: Yes . . . but let's think about the summer first.

ELIS: The summer, yes! [*He takes out his cheque-book.*] I've got the money in the bank already, you know; and as soon as term's over, we'll go up north to our own country, to Lake Malar. The cottage is all ready for us, just as it was when we were children – with the lime trees, and the punt moored under the willows. Oh I wish it were summer, and I could bathe in the lake. How I long for a lake so that I can wash myself clean, body and soul, from this shame to our family.

KRISTINA: Have you heard anything from Eleonora?

ELIS: Yes, poor child, she's unhappy – she writes me the most heart-rending letters. She wants to leave the asylum and come home, of course, but the doctor daren't let her go, because some of the things she does might get her into trouble. You know, I sometimes reproach myself terribly for agreeing to send her there.

KRISTINA: You're always blaming yourself, dear; but surely it was the best thing for her, poor child, to be properly looked after.

ELIS: Yes, you're right, of course, and I know things are better as they are. Yes, it's the best possible answer for her. She used to go about the place taking all the happiness out of everything, and when I remember what a nightmare her affliction was to us – how it drove us nearly to desperation, I'm selfish enough to be almost happy to be relieved of her. In fact, the worst thing I can imagine would be to see her walk in through that door – so you see how contemptible I am.

KRISTINA: It's only natural, dear.

ELIS: I do feel it, you know. I can't bear to think of her being unhappy, or Father either.

KRISTINA: Some people seem to be born to suffer.

ELIS: Poor Kristina, fancy coming into a family like mine – doomed from the start – and damned.

KRISTINA: Elis! You can't know if this is a punishment, or if it's sent to try us.

ELIS: I don't know which it is for you, because you are guiltless if anyone is.

KRISTINA: 'Tears in the morning mean happiness by nightfall.' Perhaps I can help you, Elis.

ELIS: Do you know if Mother has a white tie?

KRISTINA [uneasily]: Are you going out?

ELIS: Yes, I'm dining out. You see, Peter took his degree yesterday, so he's giving a dinner today.

KRISTINA: And do you really want to go?

ELIS: You mean I ought to stay away because he's turned out such an ungrateful pupil?

KRISTINA: I must admit it did upset me that, after he'd promised to quote your thesis, he was dishonest enough to steal it without acknowledging whom it came from.

ELIS: Oh, that's always happening; I'm quite content to be able to say to myself 'That's my work'.

KRISTINA: Has he invited you?

ELIS: No – you're right, he hasn't! How very odd: he's been talking about this dinner for years, as if it were taken for granted that I'd be there, and so have I. If he hasn't invited me now, it makes me look an awful fool. Oh well, it isn't the first time, and it won't be the last.

[Pause.]

KRISTINA: Benjamin's late. D'you think he'll pass his exam?

ELIS: I certainly hope so – and with honours in Latin.

KRISTINA: Benjamin's a good lad.

ELIS: Very good – a bit inclined to dream, though. You know, of course, why he's living here with us?

KRISTINA: Is it because –

ELIS: Because my father helped himself to trustee funds belonging to the boy – as he did with so many others. That's the terrible thing about it, Kristina. In school I have to see these fatherless children, whom he robbed, going through the humiliation of being charity pupils. And you can imagine how they look at me. I have to keep reminding myself of their plight, so that I can forgive their resentment.

KRISTINA: I don't believe your father is paying as dearly as you are.

ELIS: Perhaps not.

KRISTINA: We must think about next summer, Elis; not dwell on the past.

ELIS: The summer. Do you know, last night the student's voices woke me – they were singing:

'Yes, I'm coming!
Happy winds greet for me
The fields and the birds.
Tell the birch and linden,
The lake and the hill,
That I love them, and will see them once again –
See them as I saw them when I was a child.'

[*He rises, moved.*] *Shall* I really see them again? Shall I escape from this hateful town, from Ebal the Mount of Cursing, and see Mount Gerizim again?

[*He sits by the door.*]

KRISTINA: Yes, you will, you will!

ELIS: But do you think my birches and lindens will look the same to me as they did? Don't you think they'll be under the same black cloud that has lain over all nature and all life here, ever since the day when – [*He points to the arm-chair which is now in shadow*] You see! The sun has gone.

KRISTINA: But it'll come back – and stay longer.

ELIS: That's true. The days are getting longer, and the shadows are shortening.

KRISTINA: We're moving towards the light, Elis, I know we are.

ELIS: Sometimes I believe that; and when I think of the past and compare it with the present, I'm happy. Last year, you weren't sitting there; you'd broken off our engagement, and gone away. That was the hardest thing of all to bear. It was almost as if I was dying, little by little; until you came back and I began to live again. Do you remember why you went away?

KRISTINA: No, and now I look back I seem to have no reason at all. There seemed to be something inside me that told me to go, so I went – as if I were in a dream. When I saw you again, it was like waking up happy.

ELIS: And now we must never part again – because if you were to leave me now, I should really die. Here comes Mother. Don't say anything. Let her go on living in her imaginary world, where she believes that Father's a martyr and all his victims are rogues!

[MRS HEYST *comes in from the kitchen; she wears an apron and is peeling an apple. She talks in a kindly, artless way.*]

MRS HEYST: Good afternoon, children. Would you like your stewed apple hot or cold?

ELIS: Cold, please, Mother dear.

MRS HEYST: Good boy – you always know what you want and say so – and that's more than Kristina can do. Elis gets that from his father – *he* always knew just what he was doing; people don't like that, and so things went against him. But his day will come, and then they'll all see that they were wrong and he was right. Now, what was I going to say? Oh yes – did you know that Lindkvist has come to town? Lindkvist – the biggest rogue of them all!

ELIS [*getting up, excitedly*]: Has he been here?

MRS HEYST: Yes, he's staying across the street – almost opposite.

ELIS: Then, on top of everything else, we shall see him go past every day!

MRS HEYST: Give me a chance to talk to him, just once, and he'll never show his face here again. *I* know his little ways. Well, Elis, how has Peter got on?

ELIS: All right.

MRS HEYST: I knew he would. When are *you* going to take your degree?

ELIS: When I can afford to, Mother.

MRS HEYST: 'When I can afford to'? That's no answer. And what about Benjamin? Has he passed his examination?

ELIS: We don't know yet, but he'll be here any minute.

MRS HEYST: Ah . . . I don't really like the way Benjamin behaves as if he had a right to be here. Still, we'll soon cure him of that; he's a nice boy, really. Oh, by the way, Elis, there's a parcel for you.

[*She goes through the kitchen door and comes straight back with a parcel.*]

ELIS: It's funny how Mother manages to keep so up-to-date with things. I sometimes wonder if she's as simple as she makes out.

MRS HEYST: Here's the parcel – Lina took it in.

ELIS: A present! I'm rather afraid of presents ever since someone sent me a box of cobble-stones!

[*He puts the parcel down on the table.*]

MRS HEYST: Well, I'll get back to the kitchen. Aren't you cold with that door open?

ELIS: Not a bit, Mother.

MRS HEYST: Oh Elis, I wish you wouldn't hang your overcoat there, it looks so untidy. Well, Kristina, how soon will my curtains be ready?

KRISTINA: Any minute now, Mother.

MRS HEYST: Yes, I like that young Peter – he's quite a favourite of mine. Aren't you going to his dinner, Elis?

ELIS: Er – yes, of course.

MRS HEYST: Well then, why did you say you'd like your stewed apples cold, when you're going out? You really are tiresome, Elis – not like that nice Peter. Now shut that door as soon as it gets chilly, then you won't catch cold.

[*She goes out, right.*]

ELIS: She's rather an old dear. But she does go on over Peter. Is she trying to tease you about him?

KRISTINA: Me?

ELIS: You know what old ladies are – they get all sorts of ideas.

KRISTINA: What's your present?

ELIS [*ripping open the parcel*]: A branch of birch for Lent.

KRISTINA: Who's it from?

ELIS: It doesn't say. Oh well, there's no harm in that. I'll put it in water, and it will send forth shoots like Aaron's rod. 'Birch – as when I was a child' . . . And now Lindkvist has come here.

KRISTINA: Why should he upset you so?

ELIS: He's the one we owe more than anybody else.

KRISTINA: But surely *you* don't owe him anything.

ELIS: We do – we're all responsible. As long as there's a debt outstanding, it's a blot on the family's name.

KRISTINA: Change your name, then.

ELIS: Kristina!

KRISTINA [*finishing her work and putting it away*]: Dear Elis – I only wanted to make sure.

ELIS: But you shouldn't tempt me. Lindkvist is a poor man, and he needs what we owe him. Wherever my father went he left a sort of battlefield of dead and wounded – and yet Mother thinks he was unjustly treated. Would you like to go out for a walk?

KRISTINA: And try to find some sun? Yes, let's.

ELIS: Why is it that Our Redeemer suffered for our sins, and yet we must still go on paying? Nobody pays for me!

KRISTINA: But would you understand it if anybody did pay for you?

ELIS: Yes, I should understand that. Sh — here comes Benjamin. Can you see if he looks pleased?

KRISTINA [*looking out through the door at the back*]: He's walking very slowly — Now he's stopped at the fountain — he's bathing his eyes.

ELIS: That as well!

KRISTINA: You can't be sure yet.

ELIS: Always tears.

KRISTINA: Have patience.

[BENJAMIN *comes in — he is friendly and respectful, but depressed. He is carrying some books and a satchel.*]

ELIS: Well, how did you get on with the Latin?

BENJAMIN: Badly.

ELIS: Let me see your papers. What did you do?

BENJAMIN: I used the indicative with *ut* — although I knew it takes the subjunctive.

ELIS: Then you've failed! What on earth made you do that?

BENJAMIN [*meekly*]: I can't imagine. I knew the right answer, and I meant to put it down, but somehow I just wrote the wrong one.

[*He sits unhappily at the table.*]

ELIS [*settling at the desk and looking through* BENJAMIN'S *papers*]: Yes, here's the indicative. Oh Lord!

KRISTINA [*with an effort*]: Well, better luck next time. You've got all your life in front of you — and that can be a very long time.

BENJAMIN: Yes, it can.

ELIS [*sadly, but without bitterness*]: Why does everything happen at once? You were my best pupil, too, so what can I expect of the others? I shall lose my reputation as a teacher, and that'll mean no more private tuition, and then — goodness knows what I shall do. [*To Benjamin*]: Don't take it so badly — it's not your fault.

KRISTINA [*with a great effort*]: Don't lose heart, Elis — for heaven's sake, don't lose heart!

ELIS: What is there to keep me going?

KRISTINA: What there always has been.

ELIS: Things are different now – I seem to have fallen from grace.

KRISTINA: It's a sign of grace to suffer through no fault of your own. Don't let it make you bitter. This is only sent to test you, I know it is; stand up to it!

ELIS: All that won't make a year any shorter for Benjamin, will it?

KRISTINA: Yes, it will – with a happy mind, time quickly passes.

ELIS: 'Kiss the place and make it well'! That's what they tell children, isn't it?

KRISTINA: Be a child then – and listen to me. Think of your mother, and all *she* has to put up with.

ELIS: Give me your hand – I need your help. [KRISTINA *gives him her hand.*] Your hand's trembling.

KRISTINA: Surely not.

ELIS: You're not as strong as you seem.

KRISTINA: I don't feel at all weak.

ELIS: Why can't you give *me* strength, then?

KRISTINA: I suppose I've none to spare.

ELIS [*looking out of the window*]: Who do you think's coming now?

KRISTINA [*she looks through the window, and sinks brokenly to her knees*]: No! This is too much!

ELIS: Our creditor – who can seize all we possess whenever he wants to. Lindkvist, who has moved here so that he can sit like a spider in his web watching the flies.

KRISTINA: Run away!

ELIS [*getting up*]: No – we can't do that! Now that you're weakening, I'm growing strong. Look, he's coming up the street – he's got his evil eyes on this house already.

KRISTINA: Keep out of sight, at any rate.

ELIS: No – I can laugh at him now. He looks as if he's gloating to himself because he can see his prey in the trap. There now, he's counting the steps up to the gate; he can tell we're at home, because the door's open. . . . Ah, he's met someone, and he's stopping to talk to them. . . . He's looking this way, so he's talking about us!

KRISTINA: Your mother mustn't meet him – she'd only say something rash that would upset him. Don't let her, Elis.

ELIS: He's shaking his stick now! I can see from his lips what he's saying: 'This,' he declares, 'is a case for Justice rather than Mercy.' Now he's unbuttoning his overcoat – that's to show that no one's going to strip the clothes off *his* back. What can I answer? 'You're quite right sir – take all we have! It belongs to you!'

KRISTINA: There isn't much else you *can* say, dear.

ELIS: Now he's laughing. Not such a malicious laugh either. Good lord, perhaps he isn't so bad after all, even if he does mean to have his money. If only he'd finish his wretched chattering, and come in now and get it over. Ah – there goes his stick again – they always have sticks, these people who are owed money, and goloshes that go 'swish-swish' just like a cane. [*He puts* KRISTINA'S *hand on his heart.*] Feel how my heart's beating – I can hear it myself – like the throb of an ocean liner in my ears. There, he's saying 'goodbye' now, thank God – and there go the goloshes: – swish – swish – like a Lenten birch-bough. Ah, he has a watch-chain with trinkets on it – so he's not entirely destitute. They always have cornelian trinkets on their watch-chains, like bits of dried flesh cut from their neighbour's backs. Listen, to those goloshes: 'swish – swish – leech – leech – vicious – vicious – vicious!' Look out! Ah, he's seen me, he's seen me! [*He bows towards the street.*] He made the first move – he smiled, and waved his hand, and – [*He sits at the writing-desk, weeping.*] He's gone.

KRISTINA: Thank heaven.

ELIS: He's gone past – but he'll come back . . . . Let's go out into the sun.

KRISTINA: But Peter's dinner?

ELIS: Since I'm not invited, I shall stay away. Besides, what should I do among all that rejoicing? I should meet my false friend, and feel his embarrassment so much that I shouldn't be able to feel ill-used myself.

KRISTINA: I'm glad you're staying here with us.

ELIS: I'd much sooner be here – you know that. Shall we go out?

KRISTINA: Yes – let's go this way.

[*She goes out, left.*]

ELIS [*patting* BENJAMIN'S *head as he passes him*]: Cheer up, my lad.

[BENJAMIN *hides his face in his hands.*]

ELIS [*taking the birch branch from the table, and sticking it behind the mirror:*] It wasn't a sprig of olive that the dove brought, it was a birch-branch!

[*He goes.*

ELEONORA *comes in from outside. She is a girl of sixteen, with a plait down her back. She is carrying a yellow daffodil in a pot. Either she doesn't see* BENJAMIN *or she pretends not to; but going to the sideboard, she picks up the water-jug and waters the plant; then, putting it on the dinner-table, she sits there, opposite* BENJAMIN, *watching him and copying his movements.* BENJAMIN *looks at her, astonished.*]

ELEONORA [*pointing at the daffodil*]: Do you know what that is?

BENJAMIN [*with childish directness*]: Of course I do! It's a daffodil. Who are *you*?

ELEONORA [*kindly – sadly*]: Well, who are *you*?

BENJAMIN [*as before*]: My name's Benjamin, and I'm staying here with Mrs Heyst.

ELEONORA: I see. Well, my name's Eleonora, and I'm the daughter of the house.

BENJAMIN: That's funny, they've never talked about you.

ELEONORA: Oh, people never talk about the dead.

BENJAMIN: The dead?

ELEONORA: I'm dead as far as other people are concerned. You see, I did something very wicked.

BENJAMIN: *You* did?

ELEONORA: Yes, I embezzled some trustee funds – not that that mattered so much, because ill-gotten gains never prosper, but, you see, my old father was blamed for it and put in prison, and that's unforgivable.

BENJAMIN: What a funny way to talk – but I rather like it. You know, it had never occurred to me that my inheritance was ill-gotten.

ELEONORA: Man oughtn't to hold his fellow-men in bondage – he should set them free.

BENJAMIN: Well, you've set *me* free from feeling angry about having been cheated.

ELEONORA: Have you got a guardian?

BENJAMIN: Yes. It's his sorry lot to make atonement for the poor people who were ruined.

ELEONORA: You mustn't say bitter things like that, or I shall go away. I'm not strong, and I can't bear unpleasant things. But . . . have you had to suffer because of me?

BENJAMIN: Because of your father.

ELEONORA: There's no difference. We're the same person, he and I. [*Pause.*] I've been very ill. . . . Why are *you* so unhappy?

BENJAMIN: I've had a disappointment.

ELEONORA: But you oughtn't to be sorry about that: 'The rod and chastisement bringeth wisdom, and he that hateth chastisement shall die.' What was your disappointment?

BENJAMIN: I've failed in my Latin exam; I was so sure I'd get through, too.

ELEONORA: I know; you were so sure you'd get through that you were ready to bet on it.

BENJAMIN: Yes . . . I *did*, too.

ELEONORA: I thought as much. That's why you failed – because you were so sure.

BENJAMIN: Do you really think so?

ELEONORA: Of course. 'Pride goeth before a fall!'

BENJAMIN: I'll remember that, next time.

ELEONORA: Yes, you must. 'A contrite heart is an acceptable sacrifice unto the Lord.'

BENJAMIN: Are you religious?

ELEONORA: Yes, I am.

BENJAMIN: I mean – really religious.

ELEONORA: That's what *I* meant. So if you were to say a word against God, when He's been so good to me, I wouldn't sit at the same table with you.

BENJAMIN: How old are you?

ELEONORA: I don't count time or place. I'm everywhere and eternal. I'm in the prison with Father, and in the classroom with my brother; I'm in the kitchen with Mother, and in my sister's shop far away in America. When my sister's doing well – selling lots of things, then I'm happy for her, and when things go badly with her, then I'm sorry too. But I suffer most when she does something wrong. Benjamin . . . you're called Benjamin because you're the youngest of my friends – yes, everybody is my friend . . . if you'll let me look after you, then I'll be able to suffer for you too.

BENJAMIN: I don't really understand half the words you say, but I think I can see the idea behind them. I'll do whatever you want me to.

ELEONORA: Well, to begin with, you must stop judging people – even the ones who've been sent to prison.

BENJAMIN: Yes, but you must give me a reason – you see, I've been studying philosophy.

ELEONORA: Oh, have you? Then you must explain something to me that a very great philosopher once said: 'Whosoever hateth the righteous becometh himself an evil-doer'.

BENJAMIN: By all the rules of logic, it means that a man may be predestined to commit a crime.

ELEONORA: And that crime itself is a punishment.

BENJAMIN: That's very deep. It might be Kant or Schopenhauer.

ELEONORA: Might it?

BENJAMIN: What book did you find it in?

ELEONORA: In the Scriptures.

BENJAMIN: Really? Do they say things like that?

ELEONORA: What an ignorant, badly educated boy you are. If only I could bring you up!

BENJAMIN: What? A child like you?

ELEONORA: I don't think there's any real *wrong* in you, though – in fact, you look quite good. What's the name of your Latin master?

BENJAMIN: Mr Algren.

ELEONORA: I must remember that. Ah – my father's suffering now . . . they're being unkind to him. [*She stays still, as if she were listening.*] Listen to the telephone-wires singing – that's because the lovely red copper wire can't bear the wicked words that people use. When people say bad things about each other on the telephone, the wires cry out and accuse them – [*severely*] and every word is written down in the book, to be accounted for on Judgement Day.

BENJAMIN: How strict you are!

ELEONORA: No, no – *I'm* not, I shouldn't dare to be – not I! [*Going to the stove, she opens the door and takes out some torn pieces of white writing-paper.* BENJAMIN *gets up and looks at the paper, which* ELEONORA *pieces together on the dining-table. To herself*] How careless people are – leaving their secrets in the stove. Wherever I go, the first thing I do is to look in the stove. But I never do anything wrong with what I find – I shouldn't dare, or something terrible would happen to me. Now, what's this?

[*She reads.*]

BENJAMIN: It's a student called Peter, writing to ask Kristina to meet him. I've been expecting this for some time.

ELEONORA [*covering the paper with her hand*]: Oh, *you*! What have you been expecting? Tell me, you wicked boy. You see evil everywhere! There's nothing but good in this letter; you see, I know Kristina, and she's going to be my sister-in-law. This meeting will save my brother Elis from a lot of unhappiness. Benjamin, promise me you won't say a word about this?

BENJAMIN: I'm sure I shouldn't dare to speak of it.

ELEONORA: How wrong people are to have secrets. They think they're so clever, and really they're fools. What ever made me go and look there?

BENJAMIN: Yes, why are you so inquisitive?

ELEONORA: Oh well, you see, that's because of my illness – I always have to know everything, or I get upset.

BENJAMIN: Everything?

ELEONORA: I know it's a fancy, but I can't resist it. Anyhow I know what the starlings say.

BENJAMIN: They can't talk, can they?

ELEONORA: Haven't you ever heard starlings that have been taught to speak?

BENJAMIN: Oh yes, when they've been *taught*!

ELEONORA: Well then, they can learn to talk! But there are some who learn of their own accord – they're called 'natural speakers'. They sit and listen – without our knowing it, of course, and then they repeat it after us. Just now, as I came along, I heard two of them talking in the walnut tree.

BENJAMIN: You *are* a funny girl. What were they saying?

ELEONORA: Well – One of them said 'Peter' – then the other said 'Judas'. 'What's the difference?' said the first one. 'Tch, tch, tch', said the other. . . . But have you ever noticed that the nightingales only sing in the deaf-and-dumb people's garden over there?

BENJAMIN: Yes, everybody knows that. Why is it?

ELEONORA: Because people with hearing don't hear what the nightingales say, but the deaf and dumb can.

BENJAMIN: Tell me some more fairy-tales.

ELEONORA: All right, if you're good.

BENJAMIN: What do you call 'good'?

ELEONORA: Well, you mustn't ever trip me up over what I say, or tell me that I said something quite different last time. Shall I tell you more about the birds? There's a wicked bird called the rat-buzzard. As you can tell by its name, it lives on rats. But because it's a bad bird, it finds it hard to catch any rats; you see, it can only say one thing, and that sounds like a cat miaowing. And whenever the buzzard says 'miaow', the rats run and hide, but the buzzard can't see that it's because of what he's said, so he often has to go hungry, because he's such a nasty bird. Do you want me to go on? Or shall I tell you about the flowers? Do you know that when I was ill, they made me take a drug made out of henbane which has the power of turning your eyes into magnifying-glasses – Now, belladonna makes you see everything smaller. Anyhow, now I can see much farther than anyone else – I can even see the stars in broad daylight.

BENJAMIN: But the stars aren't there then!

ELEONORA: What a funny boy you are! The stars are always there. I'm facing north now, and I can see Cassiopeia like a great 'W' in the Milky Way. Can you see it?

BENJAMIN: No, I can't.

ELEONORA: Make a note of that, then: some people can see things that others can't – so don't be too sure of your own eyes. Now I'll tell you about this flower on the table; it's a daffodil, and they come from Switzerland. It has sucked the sunlight into its cup – that's what makes it so yellow, and that's how it can sooth pain. I saw it as I passed a flower-shop just now, and I wanted it for a present for my brother Elis, but when I tried to get in, I found the door was locked, because it's Confirmation Day. I simply had to have the flower, though, so I took out my keys and tried them, and – would you believe it? – my latch-key fitted, so I went in. Now, you know about the silent language of flowers? Well, every scent expresses a whole multitude of thoughts, and all those thoughts came flooding in on me; so with my magnifying eye, I looked into their laboratories where no one has ever seen before, and they told me about the pain that the clumsy gardener had caused them – I won't call him cruel, because he was only thoughtless. And then I left a krona on the counter, with my card, and I took the flower and went.

BENJAMIN: That wasn't very wise of you! Suppose they miss the flower, and don't find the money?

ELEONORA: Yes – you're right.

BENJAMIN: A coin can easily get mislaid, and if all they find is your card, then you're lost!

ELEONORA: But nobody could possibly believe that I'd want to steal anything?

BENJAMIN [*looking fixedly at her*]: No?

ELEONORA [*catching his eye, and getting up*]: Oh! Yes, I see what you mean – like father, like daughter. How careless of me! Well, what must be, must be. [*She sits.*] It can't be helped.

BENJAMIN: Can't it be put right?

ELEONORA: Sh! Let's talk about something else. . . . Mr Algren. . . . Poor Elis! Poor all of us. But it's Easter, and we must suffer. You know there's a concert tomorrow? They're playing Haydn's 'Seven Words from the Cross', 'Mother, behold thy Son.'

[*She covers her face with her hands and weeps.*]

BENJAMIN: What is this illness you have?

ELEONORA: My illness is not 'sickness unto death' but unto the glory of God. 'I looked for good, but evil came; I looked for the light, and behold, the darkness.' What was your childhood like, Benjamin?

BENJAMIN: I don't know . . . difficult. And yours?

ELEONORA: I never had any, I was born old. I was born knowing everything, and when I was taught anything, it was only like remembering. When I was four, I knew how thoughtless and inconsiderate people were – that's why they were unkind to me.

BENJAMIN: Everything you say, *I* seem to have thought of, too.

ELEONORA: You probably have. What made you think my coin in the flower-shop might be lost?

BENJAMIN: Because the worst always happens.

ELEONORA: So you've noticed that too! Sh! Someone's coming. [*She looks out at the back.*] I can hear – It's Elis. Oh I'm so glad! He's my only friend in the world. [*Becoming sombre*] But he isn't expecting me – and he won't be pleased to see me. No, he won't, he certainly won't. Benjamin – Benjamin – put on a friendly face and a cheerful expression when my poor brother comes in. I'll go out, so that you can break the news that I'm home. But no hard words that would hurt me, do you hear? Shake hands on it. [BENJAMIN *gives her his hand.* ELEONORA *kisses the top of his head.*] There! Now you're my little brother. God bless you and keep you! [*She goes out to the left, and as she passes* ELIS'S *overcoat, she gives it an affectionate pat.*] Poor Elis.

[ELIS, *looking worried, comes in from the back.* MRS HEYST *comes from the kitchen.*]

ELIS: Ah, there you are, Mother.

MRS HEYST: Was it you? I thought I heard a strange voice.

ELIS: I have some news; I met the lawyer in the street.

MRS HEYST: Well?

ELIS: The case is to go to the Court of Appeal; that means I shall have to work against time reading through all the reports of the trial again.

MRS HEYST: Well, it won't take you long.

ELIS [*pointing to the documents on the desk*]: Oh dear, I thought it was all over! Now I shall have to endure the whole painful story again – all the accusations and the evidence and the proof – all over again!

MRS HEYST: Yes, but the Court of Appeal will acquit him.

ELIS: No, Mother; he confessed.

MRS HEYST: Yes, but there may be a legal error somewhere – that was the very last thing the lawyer told me when I saw him.

ELIS: That was only to comfort you.

MRS HEYST: Aren't you going out to that dinner?

ELIS: No.

MRS HEYST: There! You've changed your mind again!

ELIS: Yes.

MRS HEYST: Oh that is tiresome of you.

ELIS: I know, but I'm being tossed about like driftwood in a storm.

MRS HEYST: I was certain I heard a strange voice – one that I recognized. I must have been wrong. [*Pointing to the overcoat*] That coat oughtn't to be hanging there – I keep telling you. [*She goes out, right.*]

ELIS [*crossing left, he sees the daffodil on the dinner-table. To* BENJAMIN]: Where did that flower come from?

BENJAMIN: A young lady brought it.

ELIS: A young lady? What young lady? Who was she?

BENJAMIN: It was –

ELIS: Was it – my sister?

BENJAMIN: Yes. [*ELIS sinks down at the table. Pause.*]

ELIS: Did you talk to her?

BENJAMIN: Oh yes.

ELIS: My God – already? Did she behave badly?

BENJAMIN: Behave badly? No, she was nice – very nice.

ELIS: How odd. Did she mention me? Was she very, very angry with me?

BENJAMIN: No – far from it. She said you were the best friend she had in the world.

ELIS: What an extraordinary change!

BENJAMIN: And as she was going she stroked the sleeve of that coat.

ELIS: Going? Where did she go?

BENJAMIN [*pointing to the door on the left*]: In there.

ELIS: She's there?

BENJAMIN: Yes.

ELIS: You look very cheerful, Benjamin.

BENJAMIN: She said such beautiful things to me.

ELIS: What did she talk about?

BENJAMIN: Oh, she told me fairy stories – and there was a lot about religion.

ELIS [*rising*]: – And it made you happy.

BENJAMIN: Yes.

ELIS: Poor Eleonora – so unfortunate herself, and yet she can make others happy. [*He goes irresolutely to the window.*] God help me!

CURTAIN

[*Overture: Haydn's 'Seven Words' — Largo No. I. Pater dimitte illis.*
The scene is the same, but the curtains are drawn, and lit outside by
the street lamp. The hanging lamp is lit, and there is a small oil-lamp
burning on the dinner-table. The fire is burning in the stove. ELIS *and*
KRISTINA *are sitting idly at the work-table; while* ELEONORA *and*
BENJAMIN *sit opposite each other at the dinner-table reading, with*
the lamp between them. ELEONORA *has a shawl round her shoulders.*
They are all dressed in black; ELIS *and* BENJAMIN *have white ties.*
The documents of the trial are spread out on the desk; the daffodil is on
the work-table, and an old clock stands on the dinner-table. From time
to time the shadow of a passer-by in the street is seen on the curtains.]

ELIS [*quietly, to* KRISTINA]: Good Friday! Yes, but what a *long*
Good Friday! And the snow is lying in the streets like straw
outside a house where someone's dying. Every sound has
stopped – except for the lowest notes of the organ – I can hear
them even here.

KRISTINA: I suppose your mother has gone to Vespers –

ELIS: Yes – she couldn't bear to go to High Mass – because of the
way people look at her.

KRISTINA: People are very strange here: they expect us to keep
ourselves apart – they think that's the proper thing.

ELIS: Perhaps they're right.

KRISTINA: But to boycott a whole family because one of them
did wrong –

ELIS: That's how things are!

[ELEONORA *pushes the lamp across to* BENJAMIN, *so that he*
can see better.]

ELIS [*pointing to* ELEONORA *and* BENJAMIN]: Look at those
two.

KRISTINA: Isn't it charming – they get on so well together.

ELIS: It's a good thing Eleonora is so quiet. I only hope it lasts.

KRISTINA: Why shouldn't it?

ELIS: Because good fortune doesn't usually last. I'm afraid of everything today.

[BENJAMIN *gently pushes the lamp towards* ELEONORA *so that she can see better.*]

KRISTINA: Look at them.

ELIS: Have you noticed how Benjamin's changed? He's lost that sulky resentment, and now he's calm and resigned.

KRISTINA: And how sweet *her* whole nature is – you'd almost call it 'beautiful'.

ELIS: She seems to have a spirit of peace about her, as if there were an unseen angel who brought tranquillity with her. Even Mother seemed quite calm when they met – so calm that I was surprised.

KRISTINA: Do you think she's cured now?

ELIS: I think so – if only she weren't so terribly sensitive still. She's sitting there reading the story of Christ's Passion, and sometimes she weeps over it.

KRISTINA: Well, I remember doing that myself when I was at school – on Wednesdays during Lent.

ELIS: Don't talk so loud – she has very sharp ears.

KRISTINA: She can't hear us – not over there.

ELIS: Have you noticed how a sort of noble dignity has appeared in Benjamin's face?

KRISTINA: Suffering does that – happiness only makes everything commonplace.

ELIS: Perhaps it might be – love. Don't you think those two young people –

KRISTINA: Sh! Sh! Sh! If you touch a butterfly's wings, it'll fly away.

ELIS: They're looking at each other – I believe they're only pretending to read – as far as I can hear, they haven't turned over any pages.

KRISTINA: Sh!

ELIS: Look – she can't sit still any longer –

[ELEONORA *gets up and, going to* BENJAMIN, *puts her shawl over his shoulders.* BENJAMIN, *after a gentle protest, gives in, and* ELEONORA *sits down again, pushing the lamp over to* BENJAMIN'S *side.*]

KRISTINA: Poor Eleonora – she doesn't realize how kind she is.

ELIS [*getting up*]: Well, I must get back to my reports of the trial.

KRISTINA: Do you think all that reading will really help?

ELIS: Yes – if only that it keeps Mother from losing hope. But even if I, too, only pretend to read, the words seem to pierce my eyes like thorns. The witnesses' evidence, the columns of figures, father's confession – things like, 'The accused admitted, with tears in his eyes . . .' Tears! So many tears! And these documents, with their stamps that make me think of forged notes or prison locks; and the tape and the red seals – like the five wounds of Jesus – and the sentences that never seem to end, like eternal torments. It's a fitting task for Good Friday. Yesterday the sun was shining, yesterday we pictured ourselves going to the country. Kristina – suppose we had to stay here all the summer!

KRISTINA: It would save us a lot of money . . . but it would be a shame.

ELIS: I should never get over it. I've spent three summers here, and it's like a tomb. Even at midday one sees the long grey street winding like a ditch, without a man or a horse or a dog! The rats come out of the sewers, because the cats are on their summer holidays! And the few people who are left here sit behind their windows, that are like mirrors, and spy on their neighbours' clothes – 'Look – that man's got his winter clothes on!' – and on their neighbours' worn shoes, and all their other defects. And from the slums, the cripples who'd kept out of sight till now, come crawling out – men without noses or ears, evil men, wretched men. And they sit and sun themselves on the great promenade, as if they owned the town. And where, a little while ago, pretty well-dressed children played, while their lovely mothers gently smiled at them, there stroll packs of ragamuffins, cursing and fighting . . . I remember one midsummer day, two years ago –

KRISTINA: Think of the future, Elis – not the past!

ELIS: Will it be any better?

KRISTINA: We must believe it will.

ELIS [*sitting at the desk*]: If only it would stop snowing, we could go out for a walk.

KRISTINA: Dear Elis! Last night you wanted the darkness again, so that we could hide from people's eyes. 'The darkness is so lovely,' you said, 'so healing . . . it's like pulling the blankets over your head!'

ELIS: There you are, you see! Things are wretched whichever way you look at them. [*He reads his papers.*] The worst thing in this trial is all the impertinent questions about Father's way of life. It says here that we gave magnificent parties – one witness says that he drank. . . .! No, it's too much, I can't go on! Yet I must – I must go on to the end. . . . Aren't you cold?

KRISTINA: No – but it's not warm in here. Isn't Lina in?

ELIS: No, she went to Communion – you know that.

KRISTINA: I suppose your mother will soon be home.

ELIS: I always dread her coming back after she's been out. She hears and sees so much – and all of it bad!

KRISTINA: There's a terrible melancholy strain in your family.

ELIS: That's why only melancholy people ever want to know us – the cheerful ones keep away.

KRISTINA: There's your mother coming in at the back door now.

ELIS: Don't be impatient with her, Kristina.

KRISTINA: Of course not. It's harder for her than for the rest of us. I don't understand her, all the same.

ELIS: She does all she can to hide her humiliation – that makes her unapproachable. Poor Mother.

MRS HEYST [*entering, she is in black, with a prayer-book and a handkerchief in her hand*]: Good evening, children.

ALL [*except* BENJAMIN, *who greets her in silence*]: Good evening, Mother dear.

MRS HEYST: You're all in black, as if you were in mourning.

ELIS: Is it still snowing?

MRS HEYST: It's turned to sleet. It's cold in here. [*She goes to* ELEONORA *and pats her.*] Well, darling, I see you're working at your lessons. [*To* BENJAMIN]: *You're* not overworking. [ELEONORA *takes her mother's hand and puts it to her lips.*]

MRS HEYST [*suppressing her emotion*]: There, there, dear.

ELIS: Did you go to Vespers, Mother?

MRS HEYST: Yes. It was the curate, and I don't like him.

ELIS: Did you see anyone you knew?

MRS HEYST [*sitting at the working-table*]: I only wish I hadn't.

ELIS: I know who that was.

MRS HEYST: Lindkvist. He came over to me –

ELIS: That was cruel of him.

MRS HEYST: He asked how things were – and you can imagine my feelings when he asked if he might call this evening.

ELIS: On Good Friday?

MRS HEYST: I didn't know what to say! And he took my silence for consent. [*Pause*] He may be here at any minute.

ELIS [*rising*]: Here? Now?

MRS HEYST: He wanted to leave a paper – he said it was urgent.

ELIS: He'll take the furniture!

MRS HEYST: He seemed so odd – I didn't know what to make of him.

ELIS: Well, let him come! He has the law on his side, and we must bow to it. We must receive him properly when he comes.

MRS HEYST: As long as I don't have to see him.

ELIS: You can stay out in the kitchen.

MRS HEYST: But he mustn't take the furniture. How could we live if he took all our things away? We couldn't live in empty rooms – we simply couldn't!

ELIS: 'Birds have nests, and foxes have holes . . .' There are homeless people who live in the forest.

MRS HEYST: Rogues may live there, not honest people.

ELIS [at the desk]: Well, I must get on with my work now, Mother.

MRS HEYST: Have you found any mistakes?

ELIS: No, I don't think there are any.

MRS HEYST: But I met the Public Notary just now, and he said there might be some technical error – a doubtful witness, an unfounded accusation, or some contradiction. You can't be reading carefully.

ELIS: I am, Mother, but it makes very painful reading.

MRS HEYST: You know, I met the Public Notary just now – oh yes, I've told you that already – and he told me there'd been a burglary in the town yesterday in broad daylight.

[ELEONORA and BENJAMIN listen.]

ELIS: A burglary in the town? Where?

MRS HEYST: It was in the flower shop in Kloster Street – but it was all very strange. They say the florist had shut his shop and gone to church because his son – or it may have been his daughter – was being confirmed. And when he came back at about three – or it may have been four, but that doesn't matter – the shop door was open and the flowers were missing – a whole lot of flowers – especially a yellow tulip – which was the first thing he missed.

ELIS: A tulip? I'm glad it wasn't a daffodil.

MRS HEYST: No, it was a tulip. Anyhow, the police are dealing with it.

[ELEONORA has risen, as if she were about to speak, but BENJAMIN goes and whispers something to her.]

MRS HEYST: Fancy breaking in during Holy Week, and while the children were being confirmed! They're all rogues in this town; that's why they put innocent men in prison.

ELIS: Do they suspect anybody?

MRS HEYST: No – but it was a peculiar thief, he didn't take anything out of the till.

KRISTINA: Oh, if only today were over!

MRS HEYST: And if Lina would only come in. Oh, I heard them talking about Peter's dinner yesterday; even the Governor was there!

ELIS: Oh? I'm surprised at that. Peter was always supposed to be against the Governor's faction.

MRS HEYST: He must have changed his mind.

ELIS: He wasn't called 'Peter' for nothing, it seems.

MRS HEYST: What have you against the Governor?

ELIS: He's an obstructionist! He obstructs everything – he obstructed the Secondary School, he obstructed the Cadet Corps, he even tried to forbid bicycles, and the wonderful plan for holiday camps. . . . And he's obstructed me.

MRS HEYST: I don't understand about all that – anyhow, it doesn't matter. The main thing is, the Governor made a speech, and Peter replied.

ELIS: – Very feelingly, I'm sure, and he denied his teacher, saying, 'I know not the man!' And straightway the cock crew. Wasn't the Governor's name Pontius, surnamed Pilate?

[ELEONORA *is about to speak, but she restrains herself.*]

MRS HEYST: You mustn't be so bitter, Elis. People are like that, and you must take them as they are.

ELIS: Listen! I can hear Lindkvist coming.

MRS HEYST: How can you hear him, with this snow?

ELIS: I can hear his stick tapping on the pavement, and his leather goloshes. You'd better go, Mother.

MRS HEYST: No, I want to stay; I have something to tell him.

ELIS: Mother dear, please go. It will be very painful.

MRS HEYST [*getting up, very much upset*]: 'Accursed be the day that I was born.'

KRISTINA: Don't curse!

MRS HEYST [*with a noble expression*]: 'Were it not more just that the unrighteous should suffer this tribulation, and the evil doer this misery.'

ELIS [*with a sudden cry of anguish*]: Mother!

MRS HEYST: My God, why hast thou forsaken me – and my children?

[*She goes out left.*]

ELIS [*listening at the window*]: He's stopped. Perhaps he thinks it's ill-mannered – or too cruel. Though I doubt it, when he was capable of writing such terrible letters! They were always on blue paper, and I've never been able to see a letter on blue paper since, without a shudder.

KRISTINA: What are you going to say to him – what will you suggest?

ELIS: I don't know. I don't seem able to think or reason. Shall I go on my knees to him, and beg for mercy? Can you hear him now? I can't hear anything except the blood pounding in my ears.

KRISTINA: Suppose the worst were to happen – if he took everything . . .

ELIS: Then the landlord would come and ask for some security – which I can't give him. He'll want it, because there won't be the furniture as security for the rent any more.

KRISTINA [*who has been looking out through the curtains*]: He's not there any more. He's gone.

ELIS: Ah. . . . You know, I'd sooner Mother was *angry* than dully resigned.

KRISTINA: She only pretends to be resigned – or perhaps she's convinced herself. Those last words of hers had something of the angry lioness about them. Didn't you feel a greatness about her?

ELIS: You know, when I think of Lindkvist now, I see him as a good-natured giant, who only wants to give the children a scare. I wonder why I should feel like that.

KRISTINA: You know how things come into your head –

ELIS: It's a good thing I wasn't at that dinner yesterday – I should certainly have made a speech against the Governor, and that would have ruined everything for me, and for all of us. Yes, that was certainly lucky.

KRISTINA: So, you see!

ELIS: Thank you for your advice. You obviously know your Peter!

KRISTINA: *My* Peter?

ELIS: Well, mine, then. Look – he's back again. Heaven help us! [*On the curtain appears the shadow of a man gradually approaching. It grows larger and larger till it is gigantic. They are all utterly terrified.*] It's the giant – it's the giant come to eat us up!

KRISTINA: Then we ought to smile – as if it were all a fairy-tale.

ELIS: I can't smile any more.

[*The shadow grows less, and vanishes.*]

KRISTINA: Then look at his stick – and you'll have to laugh.

ELIS: He's gone. Now I can breathe again, because he won't come back before the morning. Ah. . . .

KRISTINA: And in the morning, the sun'll shine, because it's the eve of the Resurrection. The snow will be gone, and the birds will sing.

ELIS: Go on talking. You make me *see* it all.

KRISTINA: If you could only see into my heart – and read my thoughts, and know that I mean well, and pray earnestly that – Elis . . . Elis, I want –

[*She stops.*]

ELIS: What? Tell me.

KRISTINA: I want – to ask you for something.

ELIS: Tell me.

KRISTINA: It's a test. Remember that, won't you? It's a test.

ELIS: A test – what sort of test? Very well.

KRISTINA: Let me – no, I daren't, it might fail.

[ELEONORA *listens.*]

ELIS: Why do you torment me?

KRISTINA: I shall regret it, I know I shall. . . . Well, so be it. Elis, let me go to the concert this evening.

ELIS: What concert?

KRISTINA: In the Cathedral; Haydn's 'Seven Words from the Cross'.

ELIS: Who with?

KRISTINA: With Alice.

ELIS: And who else?

KRISTINA: Peter.

ELIS: With Peter?

KRISTINA: There, now I've upset you. I'm sorry. But it's done now.

ELIS: So it appears. Perhaps you'll explain.

KRISTINA: I warned you that I shouldn't be able to explain — that's why I asked you to trust me absolutely.

ELIS: All right, go. I trust you; though I don't like your wanting to go out with that traitor.

KRISTINA: I realize that, but this is a test.

ELIS: One that I can't pass.

KRISTINA: You will.

ELIS: I wish I could, but I can't. But you must go, anyhow.

KRISTINA: Give me your hand.

ELIS [giving it]: Here.
  [The telephone rings.]

ELIS [at the telephone]: Hullo? There's no answer. Hullo? It's my own voice answering. Who is there? How odd, I can hear my own words, like an echo.

KRISTINA: That does happen sometimes.

ELIS: Hullo? It's uncanny. [He rings off.] Go now, Kristina — without explanations and without conditions. I shall pass the test.

KRISTINA: Do — then everything will be all right between us.

ELIS: I shall. [KRISTINA starts to go out, right.] Why are you going that way?

KRISTINA: My things are out there. Well, good-bye for the present.
  [She goes.]

ELIS: Goodbye, my dear. [Pause.] For ever.
  [He rushes out to the left.]

ELEONORA: Heaven help us, what have I done now? The police are looking for the thief, and if they find me – poor Mother, and poor Elis!

BENJAMIN [*simply*]: Eleonora – you must say that *I* did it.

ELEONORA: Can you take the blame for someone else – at your age?

BENJAMIN: It's quite easy, when you know you're innocent.

ELEONORA: But we must never tell lies.

BENJAMIN: Well, let me telephone the flower shop and tell them how it happened.

ELEONORA: No, I've done wrong, and I must be punished – with fear. I have aroused their fear of thieves, so I must suffer fear myself.

BENJAMIN: But if the police come. . . .

ELEONORA: It will be hard, but that's how it must be. Oh, if only this day would end! [*She goes to the clock on the dinner-table and moves the hands forward.*] Dear clock – do go a little faster! Tick-tock. Ping, ping, ping! Now it's eight o'clock. Ping, ping, ping! Now it's nine. Ten, eleven, twelve. Now it's Easter Saturday! Soon the sun'll be up, and then we'll write on the Easter eggs. I shall write: 'Behold, Satan has desired to get possession of thee, that he may sift thee like wheat, but I have prayed for thee.'

BENJAMIN: Why do you torture yourself so, Eleonora?

ELEONORA: I? Torture myself? Oh, Benjamin, think of all the flowers that have just opened – the anemones and the snow-drops who have to stand in the snow all day and shiver in the darkness all night. Think how they must suffer. The night's the worst, when it's dark; because they're frightened of the dark, but they can't run away – they have to stay there waiting for the daylight. Everything suffers – everything – but the flowers suffer most of all. The birds who fly here from the south, too – where are they to sleep tonight?

BENJAMIN [*simply*]: They sit in hollow trees, of course.

ELEONORA: There aren't enough hollow trees for all of them.

I've only seen two hollow trees in the park here, and they have owls living in them, who kill small birds. Poor Elis! He thinks Kristina's left him, but I know she'll come back.

BENJAMIN: If you know that, why didn't you say so?

ELEONORA: Because Elis has to suffer – everybody must suffer on Good Friday, so that they remember how Christ suffered on the Cross.

[*A police whistle is heard out in the street.*]

ELEONORA [*starting*]: What was that?

BENJAMIN [*getting up*]: Don't you know?

ELEONORA: No.

BENJAMIN: It was the police.

ELEONORA: Ah – Yes, that's how it sounded when they came and arrested father . . . and then I became ill. And now they're coming to take me.

BENJAMIN [*stationing himself facing the door, in front of* ELEONORA]: No, they shan't take you, I will protect you, Eleonora.

ELEONORA: That's kind of you, Benjamin, but you mustn't.

BENJAMIN [*looks out through the curtains*]: There are two of them. [ELEONORA *tries to push* BENJAMIN *out of the way, but he gently resists.*] No, Eleonora, *you* mustn't – if you go, I don't want to live any more.

ELEONORA: Go and sit in that chair, child. Go and sit down. [BENJAMIN *reluctantly obeys,* ELEONORA *looks through the curtains without concealing herself.*] It's only two boys! Oh we of little faith! Do you think God is so cruel, when I've done no harm – only acted thoughtlessly. That serves me right! Why did I ever doubt?

BENJAMIN: But tomorrow he'll come and take away the furniture.

ELEONORA: Let him come! Then we shall have to go. We must leave everything – all the old furniture that Father got together for us, and that I've known ever since I was a child. Yes, we oughtn't to own anything that binds us to this earth.

We must wander on the stony roads with aching feet, for the road leads upwards, that's why it is so wearisome.

BENJAMIN: Now you're torturing yourself again, Eleonora.

ELEONORA: Leave me alone. Do you know what I shall find it hardest to part from? That clock over there; it was there when I was born, and it's measured out all the hours and days for me ever since. [*She lifts the clock from the table.*] Can you hear – it's like a heart beating – just like a heart. And it stopped at the very moment my grandfather died – yes, we had it even then! Good-bye, little clock – soon you'll stop again. Do you know, when there was no luck in the house, it used to go fast – just as if it wanted to get the bad times over quickly – for *us*, of course. But when times were happy, it used to go slow, so that we could enjoy them longer. It was a kind clock. But there was an unkind one, too – that's why it has to hang in the kitchen now. It couldn't bear music, because as soon as Elis played the piano, it began to strike. We all noticed it, not just me. That's why it has to stay in the kitchen, because it was wicked. But Lina doesn't like it either, because it's noisy at night, and she can't boil eggs by it – they always turn out hard-boiled, Lina says. Now you're laughing!

BENJAMIN: How can I help it?

ELEONORA: You're a nice boy, Benjamin, but you must be serious. Think of the birch-branch behind the mirror.

BENJAMIN: But you say such funny things, I can't help smiling. Besides, why should we always cry?

ELEONORA: If we're not to weep in this vale of tears, where *can* we weep?

BENJAMIN: Ah.

ELEONORA: You'd rather laugh all day long; that's why you've suffered so. And I only like you when you're serious – remember that!

BENJAMIN: Do you think we shall get over all this, Eleonora?

ELEONORA: Yes, most of it will come right once Good Friday's over – but not all. Today the birch, tomorrow the Easter eggs. Today snow, tomorrow thaw. Today death, tomorrow resurrection.

BENJAMIN: How wise you are!

ELEONORA: Yes, I feel that it's clearing up outside already, and there's fine weather coming; the snow is melting, you can smell the thaw even in here, and tomorrow the violets will be out along the south wall. The clouds have lifted, I know they have, because I can breathe again. Oh, I know so well when the Heavens are open. Go and open the curtains, Benjamin. I want God to see us!

[*Benjamin gets up and does so; the moonlight streams into the room.*]

ELEONORA: Look! the full moon! It's the Easter moon, and now, although it's the moon that's shining, you know that the sun is still there.

CURTAIN

ACT THREE

EASTER SATURDAY

[*Prelude to this act: Haydn's 'Seven Words'. No. 5 Adagio.*
The same setting, but the curtains are open.
The scene outside is the same, but the sky is grey. The stove is lit, and the doors at the back are shut.
ELEONORA is sitting at the stove, holding a bunch of anemones. BENJAMIN comes in from the right.]

ELEONORA: Where have you been all this time, Benjamin?

BENJAMIN: I've not been long.

ELEONORA: I've been wanting you.

BENJAMIN: Where have *you* been, Eleonora?

ELEONORA: I went down to the market and bought these anemones, and now I'm going to warm them, poor little things, because they're frozen.

BENJAMIN: Where's the sun?

ELEONORA: It's behind the mist. There aren't any clouds to-day – only a sea-mist – I can smell the salt.

BENJAMIN: Did you notice if the birds were still alive out there?

ELEONORA: Yes, and not one of them shall fall to the ground save by the will of God. But in the market there were dead birds. . . .

ELIS [*coming in from the right*]: Has the newspaper come?

ELEONORA: Not yet, Elis.

[ELIS *crosses the stage – as he reaches the centre,* KRISTINA *comes in from the left.*]

KRISTINA [*without seeing* ELIS]: Has the paper come?

ELEONORA: No, it hasn't.

[KRISTINA *crosses over to the right, passing* ELIS, *who goes out, left. They do not look at one another.*]

ELEONORA: Oh, how cold it's turned! Hatred has come into

the house. As long as there was love here, we could endure anything, but now – oh, it's cold!

BENJAMIN: Why do they want the paper?

ELEONORA: Don't you understand. It'll say . . .

BENJAMIN: What?

ELEONORA: Everything! The burglary, the police – everything.

MRS HEYST [entering, right]: Has the paper come?

ELEONORA: No, Mother dear.

MRS HEYST [going out, right, again]: Let me know as soon as it comes.

ELEONORA: The paper – the paper! Oh if only the printing press had broken down, or the editor been taken ill . . . no, I mustn't say that. Do you know, I was with Father last night.

BENJAMIN: Last night?

ELEONORA: Yes, in my sleep. I was in America with my sister, too. The day before yesterday she sold thirty dollars' worth, and made five dollars profit.

BENJAMIN: Is that a lot or only a little?

ELEONORA: It's quite a lot.

BENJAMIN [slyly]: Did you meet anyone you knew, when you were in the market?

ELEONORA: Why do you ask me that? You mustn't be sly with me, Benjamin; you want to know my secrets, but you shan't.

BENJAMIN: Then don't you imagine you can learn mine that way.

ELEONORA: Listen how the telephone wires are singing. The newspaper's out now, and people are ringing up, 'Have you read it?', 'Yes, I have; isn't it terrible?'

BENJAMIN: What's terrible?

ELEONORA: Everything. Life's terrible, but we must make the best of it, all the same. Look at Elis and Kristina: they're fond of each other, and they hate each other at the same time, so that the thermometer falls when they pass through the room. She went to the concert yesterday, and today they won't speak to each other – Why? Why?

BENJAMIN: Because your brother's jealous.

ELEONORA: Don't say that word! Besides, what do you know about jealousy – except that it's an illness, and therefore a punishment; we mustn't touch evil, or it will defile us. Just look at Elis – haven't you noticed how he's changed since he started reading those papers?

BENJAMIN: About the trial?

ELEONORA: Yes. Isn't it as if all the evil in it had seeped into his soul and was showing in his face and eyes? Kristina feels it – so that the evil shan't defile her, she's put on an armour of ice. Oh, those papers! If only I could burn them! They exude malice and lies and revenge. So, my child, you must keep away from evil and impurity, both with your lips and your heart.

BENJAMIN: How clearly you see things!

ELEONORA: Do you know what would happen to me if Elis and the rest were to find out that it was I who bought the daffodil in such an odd way?

BENJAMIN: What would they do to you?

ELEONORA: I should be sent back – to the place I came from; where the sun never shines, where the walls are bare and white like a bathroom, where all you hear is weeping and wailing, and where I've already wasted a year of my life.

BENJAMIN: Where do you mean?

ELEONORA: Where men are tortured worse than in prison, the habitation of the damned, the home of tribulation, where despair watches day and night, and from which there is no escape.

BENJAMIN: Worse than prison? Where do you mean?

ELEONORA: In prison one is condemned, but *there* one is doomed. In prison one is questioned and must reply, but there they do not listen. Poor daffodil that was the cause of it all; I meant so well, and did such ill.

BENJAMIN: But why don't you go to the flower shop and say, 'This is how it happened'? You're just like a lamb being led to the slaughter.

ELEONORA: When it knows that it *must* be slaughtered, it doesn't complain or try to escape. What else can it do?

ELIS [*coming in from the left, with a letter in his hand*]: Has the paper come yet?

ELEONORA: No, Elis.

ELIS [*turning and speaking into the kitchen*]: Lina, go and buy a paper!

[MRS HEYST *comes in from the right.* ELEONORA *and* BEN- JAMIN *seem alarmed.*]

ELIS [*to* ELEONORA *and* BENJAMIN]: Go outside for a few minutes, children, would you?

[ELEONORA *and* BENJAMIN *go out left.*]

MRS HEYST: Have you had a letter?

ELIS: Yes.

MRS HEYST: From the Asylum?

ELIS: Yes.

MRS HEYST: What do they want?

ELIS: They want Eleonora back.

MRS HEYST: They shan't have her, she's my child.

ELIS: And my sister.

MRS HEYST: What do you think we should do?

ELIS: I don't know – I can't think.

MRS HEYST: *I* can! Eleonora was a child of sorrow, but she has brought happiness – though not of this world, it's true. Her unrest has been turned to peace, which she sheds on all of us. Whether she's sane or not, to me she seems wise, for she knows how to bear the burden of life better than I – or any of us. Besides, Elis, if I am sane, was I sane when I insisted on believing that my husband was innocent – when I knew all the time that he had been convicted on actual, material evidence, and that he'd even confessed? And what about you, Elis – are you in your right mind when you can't see that Kristina loves you? – When you think she hates you?

ELIS: It's a peculiar kind of love.

MRS HEYST: No, it's your conscience that chills her affection –

you're the one who hates. But you have done wrong, and so you must suffer.

ELIS: How have I done wrong? Didn't she go out with my false friend last night?

MRS HEYST: Yes, she did – and with your knowledge. But why did she go? Surely you can guess.

ELIS: No, I can't.

MRS HEYST: Very well, then you must put up with things as they are.

[*The kitchen door opens, and a hand passes the paper in;* MRS HEYST *takes it and hands it to* ELIS.]

ELIS: That was the worst thing of all. With her, I could have borne all the rest – but now my last support has been taken from me, and I must fall.

MRS HEYST: Fall, then; but fall in the right way – so that you can get up again. What's the news in the paper?

ELIS: I don't know. I'm afraid of the paper today.

MRS HEYST: Give it to me, then, and I'll read it.

ELIS: No, wait a moment.

MRS HEYST: What are you afraid of? What are you expecting?

ELIS: The very worst!

MRS HEYST: It's happened so many times already. Oh Elis, if you only knew what my life has been like – if you'd been with me, watching your father go step by step to his ruin – when I couldn't even warn all the people that he brought down with him. When the crash came, I felt like an accomplice, because I'd known of his crimes, and if the Judge had not been a reasonable man who understood how difficult things are for a wife, I should have been sentenced too.

ELIS: What brought my father down? I've never been able to understand.

MRS HEYST: Pride – as it always does.

ELIS: But we're innocent – why should we suffer for his faults?

MRS HEYST: Be quiet.

[*Pause, while she takes the paper and reads it.*]

[*At first* ELIS *stands restlessly, then paces up and down.*]

MRS HEYST: What's this? Didn't I say that — among other things — it was a yellow tulip that was stolen from the flower-shop?

ELIS: Yes, I remember it perfectly.

MRS HEYST: Here it says — 'a daffodil'.

ELIS [*alarmed*]: Does it say that?

MRS HEYST: [*sinking into a chair*]: It was Eleonora. . . . Oh, my God!

ELIS: Then it's not over yet.

MRS HEYST: It'll mean prison or the asylum.

ELIS: She can't possibly have done it — she *can't*!

MRS HEYST: Now our name will be dragged in the mud again.

ELIS: Do they suspect her?

MRS HEYST: It says that suspicion points in a certain direction — it's obvious whom that means.

ELIS: I must talk to her.

MRS HEYST [*getting up*]: Be kind to her. I can't stand any more. She was lost and found, and now she's lost again. . . . Yes, talk to her.

[*She goes out, right.*]

ELIS: Oh. . . ! [*He goes to the left door.*] Eleonora! Come here, my dear, I want to talk to you. . . .

ELEONORA [*comes in, with her hair down*]: I was just doing my hair.

ELIS: Leave it. Tell me, my dear, where did you get that flower?

ELEONORA: I took it —

ELIS: Oh, my God!

ELEONORA [*bowing her head, defeated, with her arms crossed over her chest.*]: But I left the money for it.

ELIS: You paid for it, then?

ELEONORA: Yes, and no! It's all very confusing — but I haven't done anything wrong — I only meant it for the best. Do you believe me?

164

ELIS: Yes, dear, I believe you; but the paper doesn't know that you're not to blame.

ELEONORA: Oh dear, so I must suffer for that, too — [*She bows her head, so that her hair falls over her face.*] What will they do with me now? Let them do what they like.

BENJAMIN [*coming in, left, greatly disturbed*]: No! You mustn't touch her. She's done no wrong. I know that's true, because *I* did it. *I* did it. [*He weeps.*] I did it.

ELEONORA: You mustn't believe him — it was I.

ELIS: What am I to believe — which of you?

BENJAMIN: Me.

ELEONORA: Me! Me!

BENJAMIN: Let me go to the police.

ELIS: Hush, hush!

BENJAMIN: No, I *will* go, I will!

ELIS: Quiet, children — here comes Mother.

MRS HEYST [*coming in, very excited. She takes* ELEONORA *in her arms and kisses her.*]: My child — my darling child. You have come back to me, and you shall stay with me.

ELEONORA: But you kissed me, Mother. It's years since you've done that. Why only now?

MRS HEYST: Because now — because the florist is outside, and he apologizes for causing so much trouble. They've found the lost money, and your name.

ELEONORA [*she jumps into* ELIS'*s arms and kisses him, then she puts her arms round* BENJAMIN'*s neck and kisses him on the forehead*]: Benjamin, how good of you to want to suffer for me. How could you do it?

BENJAMIN [*shyly and boyishly*]: Because I'm so fond of you, Eleonora.

MRS HEYST: Now put on your things, and go out in the garden. It's clearing up.

ELEONORA: It's clearing up. Come on, Benjamin.

[*She takes his hand, and they go out, hand in hand, left.*]

ELIS: Shall we be able to throw the birch on the fire soon?

MRS HEYST: Not yet. There's still something.

ELIS: Lindkvist?

MRS HEYST: He's outside. But he's very strange — he's so gentle. The only thing is, he talks such a lot — and all about *himself*.

ELIS: Well, now that I've seen a ray of sunlight, I'm not afraid to meet the giant. Let him come in.

MRS HEYST: Don't provoke him. Heaven has delivered our future into his hands, and the meek shall . . . well, you know where the proud go!

ELIS: I know. Listen! his goloshes, 'Woof, woof, wolf, wish'! Is he going to walk in here in them? Oh well, why not? The carpets and the furniture belong to him.

MRS HEYST: Elis — think of *us*!

[*She goes out, right.*]

ELIS: I will, Mother.

[LINDKVIST *comes in from the right. He is an elderly, serious man with a grim expression. He has grey hair, brushed up over the temples and across his pate. Large, black, bushy eyebrows; small, short, black whiskers. Round spectacles, with dark horn-rims. Large cornelian charms on his watch-chain, a cane in his hand. He is dressed in black, wearing a fur coat, and carrying a top hat; with top-boots, and leather goloshes that squeak. As he enters, he gazes curiously at* ELIS, *and he remains standing.*]

LINDKVIST: Lindkvist is my name.

ELIS [*on the defensive*]: Mine is Heyst. Please sit down.

[LINDKVIST *sits on the chair to the right of the work-table, and looks fixedly at Elis. Pause.*] What can I do for you?

LINDKVIST [*solemnly*]: Hm — Last night I announced my intention of calling on you, but on second thoughts I decided that Good Friday was not a suitable day for a business talk.

ELIS: We are much obliged.

LINDKVIST [*sharply*]: No, we are not in the least obliged. [*Pause.*] However, the day before yesterday I happened to call on the

166

Governor – [*He pauses to see what effect his words have on* ELIS.] –
do you know the Governor?

ELIS [*casually*]: I haven't the honour.

LINDKVIST: Then you shall have the honour! We talked about
your father.

ELIS: I'm sure you did.

LINDKVIST [*he produces a paper which he puts on the table*]: And I
got this paper from him.

ELIS: I've been expecting this for a long time. But, before we go
any further, may I ask you a question?

LINDKVIST [*curtly*]: Please do.

ELIS: Why don't you take this paper direct to the Official Re-
ceiver, then at least we should avoid this long and painful
ordeal.

LINDKVIST: So that's how you feel, young man?

ELIS: I may be young, but I'm not asking for mercy, only justice.

LINDKVIST: Exactly – not mercy, only justice. Look at this
paper that I put on the table, here. Now I'm putting it away
again. You shall have justice, only justice. Now, my friend,
listen: once upon a time, I was robbed – robbed of my money,
in a most unpleasant way. When I wrote to you, quite
pleasantly, asking how much respite you needed, you
answered me rudely. You treated me as if I were a usurer who
wanted to plunder the widow and orphan, although I was the
one who had been plundered, and you were on the side of the
robbers. However, I was more considerate, and I contented
myself with a polite, but firm, reply to your ill-mannered
abuse. You recognize this blue paper of mine, eh? I can have
it stamped whenever I wish; but at the moment, I don't wish.
[*He looks round the room.*]

ELIS: Look round by all means – the furniture is at your disposal.

LINDKVIST: I wasn't looking at the furniture, I was looking to
see if your mother was there. She presumably loves justice as
much as you do.

ELIS: I hope so.

LINDKVIST: Good. Do you realize that if the justice you set such store by had run its course, your mother might have been convicted as an accomplice.

ELIS: Oh no!

LINDKVIST: Yes — and it is not too late even now.

ELIS [*rising*]: My mother!

LINDKVIST [*taking out another paper, also blue, and putting it on the table*]: Now look. Here's another paper on the table — really blue this time — also not stamped yet.

ELIS: Oh God . . . Mother! It's all come full circle —

LINDKVIST: Yes, my young lover of justice, it all comes full circle, everything — that's how things are. If I were to ask myself, 'Now, Anders Johan Lindkvist, born in poverty and brought up in want and drudgery, is it right that, in your old age, you should deprive yourself and your children — mark that: *your* children — of the support which by your industry, forethought, and self-denial — mark that: self-denial, you have saved up, copper by copper? What would you do, Anders Johan Lindkvist, if you wanted to be just? You never robbed anyone, but if you don't want to go on being robbed, then you won't be able to live in towns any more, because no one will associate with a man who's hard-hearted enough to demand his own property back. So you see, there is a charity that contradicts the law and supersedes it — and that is mercy.

ELIS: You are right. Take everything, it belongs to you.

LINDKVIST: I have the right, but I dare not exercise it.

ELIS: I shan't complain, I shall think of your children.

LINDKVIST [*putting the paper away*]: Good. Then we can put the blue paper away again. Now we'll go a step further.

ELIS: Just a moment — are they really going to prosecute my mother?

LINDKVIST: First, let us go a step further. So you don't know the Governor personally?

ELIS: No, and I don't want to know him.

LINDKVIST [*takes out the blue paper again and waves it*]: Come,

come! You see, the Governor was a school-friend of your father's, and he would like to get to know you. It all comes full circle, you see. Won't you go and see him?

ELIS: No.

LINDKVIST: The Governor –

ELIS: Let's change the subject.

LINDKVIST: You ought to be polite to me, because I'm quite defenceless – you see, you have public opinion on your side, and I have only justice. What have you against the Governor? He doesn't like bicycles and secondary schools – those are little fads of his. We need not exactly agree with them, but we can ignore them – ignore them, and go to the heart of the matter – as man to man. In the great crises of life, we must take each other with all our faults and weaknesses – swallow each other whole, as it were. Go to the Governor!

ELIS: Never!

LINDKVIST: Is that the sort of man you are?

ELIS [*firmly*]: It is!

LINDKVIST [*getting up and beginning to pace about the room in his squeaky boots – waving the blue paper*]: That's bad – worse than ever! Very well, I'll try another way. . . . There's a vindictive person who means to bring a charge against your mother. You can stop him.

ELIS: How?

LINDKVIST: Go to the Governor!

ELIS: No.

LINDKVIST [*going to Elis and seizing him by the shoulders*]: Then you're the most contemptible person I've ever met. And now I'm going to see your mother myself.

ELIS: Don't do that!

LINDKVIST: Then will you go to the Governor?

ELIS: I will.

LINDKVIST: Say that again – louder.

ELIS: I will.

LINDKVIST: Then that's settled. [*He puts down the blue paper.*]

There's *this* paper. [ELIS *takes the paper, without reading it.*] Now we come to the second point – which was the first. . . . Shall we sit down? [*They sit, as before.*] You see, if only we could meet each other half-way, it would be easier for both of us. Now, Point Number Two – my claim to your home. But make no mistake about it, I cannot give away what belongs to my whole family, nor will I. I shall press my claim to the last farthing.

ELIS: So I understand.

LINDKVIST [*sharply*]: Oh? You understand, do you?

ELIS: I didn't mean it rudely.

LINDKVIST: No, I realize that. [*He raises his spectacles and looks at* ELIS.] Wolf! Ravening wolf! Whip-lash! With flesh-coloured cornelians! The giant from the Skinnarviksberg who doesn't eat children, but only frightens them. I shall frighten you, indeed, frighten you out of your wits, I shall. I'll have full value for every stick of furniture – I have the inventory in my pocket, and if a single stick is missing, you'll go to prison, where you won't see the sun *or* Cassiopeia! Yes, I can eat children – and widows too, when they annoy me. And as for what people will say – pah! I can simply move to another town. [ELIS *is speechless.*] You have a friend called Peter – Peter Holmblad – a student of languages, and your pupil. But you tried to make him into some sort of disciple. Well, he was faithless, the cock crowed twice, didn't it? [ELIS *is silent.*] Human nature is unreliable, like all mind and matter. Peter *was* faithless, I don't defend him – not on that point. But the human heart is unfathomable – a mixture of gold and dross. Peter was a faithless friend, but he was a friend none the less.

ELIS: Faithless –

LINDKVIST: Faithless, but none the less a friend. This faithless friend, unknown to you, has done you a great service.

ELIS: That too?

LINDKVIST [*moving nearer to* ELIS]: Everything comes full circle in the end – everything.

ELIS: Everything evil, yes; and the good is repaid with evil.

LINDKVIST: Not always. The good also comes back, take my word for it.

ELIS: I shall have to, or you'll plague the life out of me.

LINDKVIST: Not your life, but I would force out your pride and your malice.

ELIS: Go on.

LINDKVIST: I tell you Peter has done you a service.

ELIS: I won't accept any service from that man.

LINDKVIST: So we're back at that again! Now, listen to me: thanks to your friend Peter's persuasion, the Governor was induced to intervene on your mother's behalf. Therefore you must write to Peter and thank him. Promise me that.

ELIS: No! To anyone else in the world, but not to him!

LINDKVIST [*pulling him nearer*]: So I shall have to press you still further, eh? Very well – you have some money in the bank?

ELIS: What business is that of yours? I'm not responsible for my father's debts.

LINDKVIST: Aren't you? Aren't you? Weren't you there, eating and drinking, when my children's money was being squandered here in this house? Answer me that.

ELIS: I can't deny it.

LINDKVIST: Then since the furniture is not enough to pay the debt, you will make out a cheque for the balance at once – you know the amount.

ELIS [*crushed*]: Even that?

LINDKVIST: Even that! Please write the cheque. [ELIS *rises, takes out a cheque-book, and writes at the desk.*] Make it out to 'Bearer'.

ELIS: It still won't be enough.

LINDKVIST: Then you must go and borrow the rest – to the last farthing!

ELIS [*giving the cheque to* LINDKVIST]: Here it is – everything I possess. It's my summer and my bride; there's nothing more I can give.

LINDKVIST: Then go and borrow, I tell you.

ELIS: How can I?

LINDKVIST: You must find a surety.

ELIS: No one would stand surety for a Heyst.

LINDKVIST: Then here's my ultimatum: you have two alternatives – either thank Peter, or pay the full amount.

ELIS: I'll have no dealings with Peter!

LINDKVIST: Then you're the most despicable creature I know. By an act of common courtesy you could save your mother's home, and your fiancée's future, and you will not do it. You must have some hidden motive. Why do you hate Peter?

ELIS: Kill me, but don't torture me any more!

LINDKVIST: You're jealous of him. [ELIS *shrugs his shoulders.*] So *that's* it! [*He rises and paces up and down. Pause.*] Have you read the paper this morning?

ELIS: Yes – unfortunately.

LINDKVIST: Right through?

ELIS: No, not every word.

LINDKVIST: Ah! Then – you don't know that Peter is engaged?

ELIS: No, I didn't know.

LINDKVIST: Nor to whom? Guess.

ELIS: How can – ?

LINDKVIST: He's engaged to Miss Alice. It happened last night at a certain concert, and your fiancée acted as go-between.

ELIS: Why all this secrecy?

LINDKVIST: Haven't two young people the right to keep such an intimate secret from you?

ELIS: And must I suffer like this for their happiness?

LINDKVIST: Yes. Others have had to suffer for your happiness. Your mother, your father, your sweetheart, your sister. Sit down, and I'll tell you a story – only a short one. [ELIS *sits, reluctantly. The weather, which has been lifting for some time, clears during the following scene.*] It happened about forty years ago. I came to the capital as a young man, alone, unknown and without friends, to look for work. It was a dark night and I only had one kroner. As I didn't know of any cheap hotel, I asked the passers-by, but no one would answer. Then, when I was in the depths of despair, a man came and asked me why I was crying – for there were tears in my eyes. When I told him my troubles, he went out of his way to take me to an hotel, and made friendly conversation to cheer me up. As I came into the vestibule, the glass door of a shop opened suddenly, hitting me on the elbow, and breaking the glass. The angry shop-keeper stopped me and threatened to call the police unless I paid for the damage. You can imagine how I felt, at the thought of spending a night in the streets. My unknown friend, who had seen the whole thing, intervened, and even took the trouble to go and see the police himself, and so saved me. That man . . . was your father! So everything comes full circle – the good things as well. And for your father's sake, I have withdrawn my claim. So – take this paper, and keep the cheque. [*He rises.*] As you seem to find it hard to say 'Thank you', I shall go now – especially as it embarrasses me to be thanked. [*Going to the door at the back.*] Now go to your mother at once and put her mind at rest. [ELIS *tries to go to him, but he waves him back.*] Go on. [ELIS *hurries out to the right. The door at the back opens and* ELEONORA *and* BENJAMIN *enter, calm but serious. They stop in alarm as they see Lindkvist.*] Well, young people! Don't be frightened; come in! You know who I am. [*In an assumed voice*]: I am the giant from the Skinnarviksberg, who frightens children. Booh! But I'm not really dangerous. Come here, Eleonora! [*Taking her head between his hands, he looks into her eyes.*] You have your father's kind eyes . . . he was a good man, but weak. [*He kisses her on the forehead.*] There!

ELEONORA: Oh! He speaks well of Father. Can anyone think well of him?

LINDKVIST: *I* can. . . . Ask your brother Elis.

ELEONORA: Then you don't want to harm us?

LINDKVIST: No, dearest child.

ELEONORA: Then help us!

LINDKVIST: My child, I can't help your father to escape from his punishment, or Benjamin from his Latin examination. But I have already helped with the rest. Life can't give you everything, and it gives nothing free; so you must help me. . . . Will you?

ELEONORA: But I'm so poor, what can *I* do?

LINDKVIST: What is the date today — look and see.

ELEONORA [*taking the calendar from the wall*]: It's the 16th.

LINDKVIST: Well, before the 20th, you must make your brother Elis both go and call on the Governor and also write a letter to Peter.

ELEONORA: Is that all?

LINDKVIST: What a child you are? But if he doesn't do it, the Giant will come and say Booh!

ELEONORA: Why does the Giant come and frighten children?

LINDKVIST: To make the children good.

ELEONORA: That's true — the Giant is quite right. [*She kisses the sleeve of* LINDKVIST'*s fur coat.*] Thank you, nice Giant.

BENJAMIN: You must call him 'Herr Lindkvist', you know.

ELEONORA: No — that sounds so ordinary.

LINDKVIST: Goodbye, children. Now you can throw the birch onto the fire.

ELEONORA: No, let it stay where it is — children forget so quickly.

LINDKVIST: How well you know children, little one. [*He goes.*]

ELEONORA: Benjamin! We can go to the country — in two month's time. Oh, if only the time would pass quickly! [*She tears the pages off the calendar, and scatters them in the shaft of sunlight that streams into the room.*] See how the days fly. . . . April . . . May . . . June . . . And — look, the sun shines on all of them! Now you must thank God for helping us to get to the country.

BENJAMIN [*shyly*]: Can't I say it to myself?

ELEONORA: Yes, you can say it to yourself, for the clouds have gone now, so it will be heard in Heaven.

[KRISTINA *has come in and stands at the left and* ELIS *and* MRS HEYST *at the right.* KRISTINA *and* ELIS *approach each other with love in their eyes, but before they can meet, the curtain falls.*]